What Your Colleagues Are S

Are you wondering how to have conversations with your youngest learners about essential topics for today's classrooms? In *Rebellious Read Alouds*, Vera Ahiyya will support you every step of the way beginning with her accessible three-part framework—start small, be consistent, be constant. In each lesson, she skillfully weaves together literacy and social justice standards without losing sight of your primary focus—learners. Every rebellious read aloud includes key questions to spark conversation and action. With Vera whispering in your ear, you'll feel confident in taking steps toward "activating your young activists."

—**Maria Walther**, Author
The Ramped-Up Read Aloud and *Shake Up Shared Reading*

I have spent decades promoting the art and function of read aloud experiences and have been a staunch advocate for revisiting books with a different lens to provide students opportunities to unearth nuance, shift perspective, build empathy, and take action. As I was reading *Rebellious Read Alouds*, I found myself nodding and saying, "amen," a lot. If you believe that small children cannot be part of big conversations, this book is for you. If you find "hushed" topics uncomfortable, this book is for you. If you are searching for books that can spark interest and action for social justice, this book is for you. If you are searching for a way to bring read aloud, deep conversations, big thinking, and the growth of human potential into your classroom while addressing the "have tos" of school, this book is for you. As you read, you have Vera Ahiyya there with you, nudging, encouraging, and offering scaffolds to help you take the next step. The author has curated an impressive list of books around nine themes that are general enough to fit in almost any elementary classroom. She has developed 45 lessons (enough for each week of the school year with a bonus lesson within each theme) that are organized around a simple framework (start small, be consistent, keep constant) that can be generalized to any theme you may choose to pursue. I'll say it again, this book is for you.

—**Lester Laminack**
Educator, Author, and Consultant

I will be sharing Vera Ahiyya's book with all my preservice and early career teachers, who understand the importance of filling their classroom libraries with books that serve as windows, mirrors, and sliding glass doors. Vera empowers us with manageable and engaging ways to use books as the springboard for the essential—though often tricky-to-start—conversations about race, ability, and so many other areas of identity. She encourages rebellion in the best possible way—to ensure that all children are seen and valued in classrooms.

—**Molly Ness**, Author
Every Minute Matters and *Think Big With Think Alouds, Grades K–5*

Vera Ahiyya has created something amazing for every stage of the rebellious reader's heart! The power of a great story is that it can be the catalyst to so much change. In *Rebellious Read Alouds*, Ahiyya beautifully breaks down stories, lessons, and ideas about books that inspire the most important conversations, the conversations about who we are. The framework of *Rebellious Read Alouds* effortlessly empowers educators and parents to start using literacy to better understand their world and themselves. This book is a must read for all.

—**Juan E. Gonzalez Jr.**
Elementary School Teacher, Speaker, and Social Media Content Creator

As I read the manuscript, I kept thinking to myself, this a book teachers need in their hands. So many teachers don't know how to read and talk about these topics and this is the guide to help them. The breadth of diversity is overflowing, and teachers can follow along with a sample scope and sequence *or* pick and choose topics and books as they see fit. Vera Ahiyya's passion for the subject rings through and her voice is loud and clear.

—**Matt Halpern**
Education Consultant, Speaker, and Author

One of the most important aspects of professional learning is that the experience not only explains *why* it's important to make an instructional shift but also *how* to do so. *Rebellious Read Alouds: Lessons to Invite Conversations About Diversity With Children's Books* is one of those precious gifts for teachers that is both inspirational and practical in a way that is empathetic and responsive to and supportive of the needs of teachers and students. Vera Ahiyya provides the *why*—rationale for being rebellious as a teacher and interviews with featured educators—as well as the *how*, with standards-based read aloud lessons that show teachers how to make necessary shifts to instructional practices that use a framework of *the small, the consistent, and the constant* as a scaffold. In these pages, we see what it looks like to partner with parents, administrators, and colleagues along the way, and how to make the journey both enjoyable and transformational for teachers and students as a community of learners.

—**Afrika Afeni Mills**
DEI Director, Educational Consultant, and Author
Open Windows, Open Minds: Developing Antiracist, Pro-Human Students

Are you ready to break free from the confines of what may sometimes seem like stale literature not representative of the world around us, but more important, the world of our children? *Rebellious Read Alouds* is a must-read for anyone and everyone lucky enough to stare into young eyes full of wonderment and a thirst to learn about their peers around them. Ahiyya Vera provides an invitation to venture into what many naively still view as uncharted territory in children's literature. *Rebellious Read Alouds* boldy—and responsibly!—provides title after title of literature that serve as catalysts for dialogue and are rooted in topics that are beautifully a part of our children's lives: immigration, divorce, religion, LGBTQ+, and others, all while promoting an environment of celebration and appreciation of the beauty of our differences. As global educators, we have the responsibility to interrupt and dispel stereotypes and ignorant ideologies that often run rampant in the world around us, and instead instill awareness, compassion, and acceptance of others so that our children may engage with their community and beyond to make our planet more peaceful, sustainable, and equitable.

—**Hilda E. Martinez**
2020 San Diego County Teacher of the Year, Early Literacy Resource Teacher

Rebellious Read Alouds is a book that is needed right now and it's presented in a way that is simple, easy to use, and yet has a strong call to action for the urgency of this work in our world today. Children deserve to have teachers who honor the identity of all children in their classrooms and beyond and the author shows us how this is possible with read aloud books and powerful conversations. This book is an excellent entry point for brave teachers to do the work.

—**Katie Keier**, Kindergarten Teacher and Co-author
Catching Readers Before They Fall

This beautiful and impactful guide will change the pedagogical approach of educators worldwide. Vera Ahiyya's overall theme is to create a true safe space for students and all involved to come face to face with their deepest emotions, fears, and ultimately reflections in the mirror via read alouds. By doing this, educators, parents, and community members will be challenged to do the same as they learn the importance of taking time to connect with your students, embracing diverse perspectives to inspire change beyond the classroom through creative critical reflection, thanks to this text.

—**Darius Phelps**
GAEYC 2016 Childcare Giver of the Year, Educator, Writer, Poet, and Illustrator

Vera Ahiyya is the QUEEN of books for a reason! This book is for any teacher who wants to center inclusiveness and diversity but isn't always sure where to start. The author has taken the time to carefully cultivate a list of books that you should be reading and walks you through how to tackle the lessons and topics that some might find controversial or intimidating.

—**Naomi O'Brien**
Founder of Read Like a Rock Star, Content Creator, and Author

Rebellious Read Alouds

Rebellious Read Alouds

Inviting Conversations About Diversity With Children's Books

Vera Ahiyya

FOR INFORMATION:

Corwin

A SAGE Company

2455 Teller Road

Thousand Oaks, California 91320

(800) 233-9936

www.corwin.com

SAGE Publications Ltd.

1 Oliver's Yard

55 City Road

London EC1Y 1SP

United Kingdom

SAGE Publications India Pvt. Ltd.

B 1/I 1 Mohan Cooperative Industrial Area

Mathura Road, New Delhi 110 044

India

SAGE Publications Asia-Pacific Pte. Ltd.

18 Cross Street #10-10/11/12

China Square Central

Singapore 048423

President: Mike Soules

Vice President and Editorial
    Director: Monica Eckman

Executive Editor: Tori Mello Bachman

Content Development Editor: Sharon Wu

Editorial Assistant: Nancy Chung

Project Editor: Amy Schroller

Copy Editor: Sarah J. Duffy

Typesetter: C&M Digitals (P) Ltd.

Proofreader: Lawrence W. Baker

Indexer: Sheila Hill

Cover Designer: Scott Van Atta

Marketing Manager: Margaret O'Connor

Printed in the United States of America

Library of Congress Cataloging-in-Publication Data

Names: Ahiyya, Vera, author.

Title: Rebellious read alouds : inviting conversations about diversity with children's books, grades K-5/ Vera Ahiyya.

Description: Thousand Oaks, California : Corwin, 2022. | Series: Corwin literacy | Includes bibliographical references and index.

Identifiers: LCCN 2021059496 | ISBN 9781071844144 (paperback) | ISBN 9781071876800 (epub) | ISBN 9781071876794 (epub) | ISBN 9781071876787 (pdf)

Subjects: LCSH: Oral reading. | Picture books for children—Educational aspects. | Social justice in education. | Language arts (Elementary) | Children—Books and reading.

Classification: LCC LB1573.5 .A55 2022 | DDC 372.45/2—dc23/eng/20220106
LC record available at https://lccn.loc.gov/2021059496

This book is printed on acid-free paper.

22 23 24 25 26 10 9 8 7 6 5 4 3 2 1

CONTENTS

3

PART THREE: Communicating With Parents, Administrators, and Colleagues
135

For downloadable resources, video interviews,
and other materials related to
Rebellious Read Alouds—including a bonus lesson set—
visit the companion website at
resources.corwin.com/rebellious.

PROLOGUE

I have a deep passion for teaching, having come from a long line of educators. There's a school in Balch Springs, Texas, named after my great grandfather, in fact. Many years ago, he was the janitor, bus driver, teacher, and principal at a small school outside of Mesquite, Texas. His strong work ethic inspired his nine children, which included my grandfather, to attend college, pursue a career they were passionate about, and keep family first. My grandfather, after a career in the military, retired and decided to follow in his father's footsteps. He became a math teacher, then later a high school assistant principal. My grandmother, his wife, attended Bowie State University in Maryland (an HBCU) and, after graduation, started her career in education. She began her career as a physical education teacher and later became a first-grade teacher. While teaching, she and my grandfather raised six children. Of the six, two pursued careers in education: my aunt, who was a math teacher, an elementary school principal, and later a college professor, and my mother, a high school English language arts teacher, who later became a coordinator for school improvement (assistant principal) and, before she retired, an executive director for Region 3 in El Paso, Texas.

My mother graduated from high school at age 15, then graduated from college at 18, and immediately began her teaching career. Because my mother was an English teacher, many of my childhood memories center around reading. I remember memorizing lines from various Shakespeare plays while my friends recited lines from their favorite cartoons. As an only child, there was very little that I wasn't allowed to get away with. I wasn't spoiled per se, but I did get what I wanted most of the time. And what I wanted most was books.

If I go back to my hometown of El Paso, many of my longtime friends reminisce on my love of books. "You would always be sitting in a corner with your nose in a book," they say. I was never a fan of the *Baby-Sitter's Club*; instead, I preferred books like *Fear Street* or *Goosebumps*. I loved reading scary stories mostly for the thrill of what could possibly happen next, the anticipation. But I think there was another reason I gravitated to these stories more than others: there was no real indication of the race or ethnicity of the characters. Yes, there was a cover that typically featured a white character, but spooky books never focused on the characters' race, just on how they would escape frightening or tense situations. I could be a part of the story because there was no reason why it couldn't be me running through my school trying to escape from an evil ventriloquist dummy.

So, while I devoured books, I can barely recall "seeing" myself in those books. When I became a teacher and read Rudine Sims Bishop's (1990) quote about books being mirrors and windows, I knew that providing those experiences would be of the utmost importance in my classroom. I wanted to find a way for students to feel the excitement and joy of reading *and* feel connected to the story. Students of marginalized groups should not have to pick one or the other. They deserve it all.

In this book, I want to show you how you can help the students in your classroom see themselves and their peers in the books you read together and independently—and I want to show you how adding diversity to your classroom read alouds can lead to deep, thoughtful conversations about race, gender, identity, religion, ability, and more. In this book, I share with you some of my favorite children's books written or illustrated by people in traditionally marginalized populations: Black, Latinx, Indigenous, Asian, LGBTQIA+, those who practice a religion other than Christianity, folks who live with disabilities, and more. And I'll show you how you can invite, spark, and manage conversations around these books and their important topics with your elementary students.

This might seem overwhelming. I bet you're a little nervous and your heart rate just went up a bit. Thinking about talking to young children about race (or any "hushed" topic) when you've never had these conversations before is intimidating. Here are a few steps to help you prepare:

*Share these books with family and friends. Practice the potential conversations you'll have with people you know and trust first, before inviting conversations with students.

*Do a bit of research and reflection. Did you know young children can start to identify different races as young as three years old? Do you know the difference between gender and gender expression? How do you honor and celebrate different holidays and traditions in your classroom or at your school? What holidays does your school offer time off for, and what traditions does your school celebrate? Did you know that Black girls are often perceived as less innocent, and therefore maybe they are less likely to receive mentorship or leadership opportunities in school? When you begin to understand the ways gender, language, stereotypes, bias, race, and racism present in school and society—and how this affects children from an early age—you'll begin to understand the necessity of these conversations.

*Think of the small, the consistent, the constant. Consider how overwhelming it can feel to be awakened to the urgency of some of these topics, so break conversations into workable, meaningful chunks:

Here are some great resources to lead you along the journey:

"Children Are Not Colorblind: How Young Children Learn Race" (article by Erin N. Winkler, PhD): https://bit.ly/3jQFUbl

"Girlhood Interrupted: The Erasure of Black Girls' Childhood" (article by Rebecca Ebstein, Jamilia J. Blake, and Thalia González): https://bit.ly/2Y5Hy19

"Black Adolescent Girls: Do Gender Role and Racial Identity Impact Their Self-Esteem?" (article by Tamara Buckley and Robert T. Carter): https://bit.ly/3whYy0t

"Promoting Self-Esteem Among African-American Girls Through Racial, Cultural Connections" (article by Kim Eckart): https://bit.ly/3CBICc7

"Anti-Bias Education and Holidays: Making Thoughtful Decisions" (article by Louise Derman-Sparkes and Julie Olsen Edwards): https://bit.ly/3nLNNQj

"A Note on Language: The Gender Unicorn" (article by the Ontario Ministry of Children, Community and Social Service): https://bit.ly/3jXZHWf

- Start small. What did we learn from this story?

- Be consistent. Who is telling the story, and who do we not see?

- Keep constant. What's our plan of action? What do we do with what we've learned?

The lessons throughout this book are organized around the small, the consistent, and the constant. These questions can help guide your thinking and your conversations with children.

It's one thing to have a collection of books that feature diverse characters; it's another, maybe more important thing to engage your students in powerful conversations around what they just read. The following pages will prepare you for some of those conversations. We center our conversations around a picture book, and pull out all the best parts, so you can be sure you hit your learning standards, engage your students in new thinking, and help them start to take action to make this world a better place.

With our rebellious read alouds, we push against the traditional and create a new normal where we can help every student feel valued, seen, and respected. I dream of a time when we don't even use the word *diverse* to describe books written by and featuring traditionally marginalized people. In fact, when titling this book, I decided not to include the term *diverse books* because it inadvertently centers our gaze on white, heteronormative, ableist thinking. May the conversations around beautiful children's literature allow us all to take steps toward realizing that time when we can celebrate diversity simply because it's who we are, not because it's "other."

ACKNOWLEDGMENTS

There are so many people to acknowledge and thank for their support and love while I wrote this book.

This list can, in no way, ever express my love and gratitude for everyone's support. But here's a start:

- My husband. You are my biggest supporter. You believe in me when I don't. You encourage me when I am exhausted. You have seen so much of what I am, before I even knew it. I can never thank you enough. Bing bong.

- My family. My inspiration. My purpose. Everything I do is to honor you. To continue a legacy of purpose, activism, and inspiration is something I strive for every day. I hope I have made you all proud.

- My mother. Thank you for putting books in my hands. Thank you for encouraging me to read anything that made me happy. Thank you for being the reason I am the person I am today.

- My friends. I am so lucky to know you. Each of you makes me better. Thank you for always supporting me, helping me, and encouraging me.

- My students. I hope each of you sparks your own rebellion. I want nothing more than for you to find your voice and use it to make the best kind of change possible. Each of you is my hope and inspiration for a better future. Be rebellious.

- To the authors and illustrators I have featured in this book, I could not have done this without you. Literally. Thank you for pouring your heart and soul into your work and sharing your gifts with all of us. Each of these titles means so much to me, and I am forever grateful for your talents.

- To Tori, Sharon, Nancy, and the rest of the (extremely supportive and wonderful) Corwin team. Thank you from the bottom of my heart for believing in me and this work. Thank you for the time and energy you poured into *Rebellious Read Alouds* to make it exactly the book I dreamt it could be.

- To you, the rebellious reader reading these pages, thank you for believing in a world where *every* child is seen, respected, loved, and cared for. Thank you for starting a rebellion in your classroom.

Let's get rebellious.

PUBLISHER'S ACKNOWLEDGMENTS

Melissa Black
Elementary Teacher
District of Columbia Public Schools

Matt Halpern
Educational Consultant/Presenter/Author

Katie Keier
Kindergarten Teacher, Adjunct Professor
Fairfax County Public Schools, American University

Darius Phelps
Middle Grades Teacher, PhD Student in English Education
Teachers College, Columbia University

ABOUT THE AUTHOR

Vera Ahiyya (née Corbett) was born in Germany and raised in El Paso, Texas. Originally a pre-med student, Vera realized her calling as an educator at Austin College in Sherman, Texas, a calling shared by many in her family, including her beloved Papa. For her BA, Vera majored in history and psychology, and she earned her MA in education. Vera has taught kindergarten and first grade for sixteen years in Texas, Massachusetts, and New York.

Vera's love for children's books has led to her becoming an Instagram book influencer, where she showcases her love of children's literature and highlights books and authors that discuss the necessity for and power of diversity and voice in children's books. She uses her extensive online presence to advocate for teachers to be purposeful and always inclusive with their choice of text in their classrooms.

Following a video showing her discussing racism with her kindergarten class that went viral and was shown on *Good Morning America*, Vera was approached to write her first children's book, *You Have a Voice,* which published in December 2021. She has other titles in the works.

Vera lives in Brooklyn with her husband Lonnell and dog Mozi. You can find her on Instagram at @thetututeacher.

This book is dedicated to anyone who has made and will make good trouble.

"Speak up, speak out, get in the way. Get in good trouble, necessary trouble."

—John Lewis

PART ONE

What Is a Rebellious Read Aloud?

So, when we talk about rebellious read alouds, what are we rebelling against exactly?

We are rebelling against what we have been told are the norms: The norm that says that early elementary students are too young to have important conversations. The norm of a white Eurocentric curriculum that tells only one side of a very important story. The norm of a nuclear family. The norm of colorblindness. The norm that says disability means helplessness. The norm that says "you can't do/say that" in public schools.

We are rebelling against all the ways in which we've been told to stay quiet, to ignore, or to dismiss.

Instead, we are pushing through. We are traveling down a path that shakes up the norm. It is loud, it is thoughtful, it is inclusive, it is rebellious. And it can start with something as simple as a children's book.

A rebellious read aloud...

- Provides an opportunity to explore deeper conversations around "hushed" topics that are typically spoken in a whisper or quiet voice: "Oh, that child has *two dads*," or "You know Jessica, the *Black girl*." Many of us are afraid to talk about hushed topics. Yet hushed topics are some of the most important to build conversations around because no one's identity should be whispered.

- Features characters that are accurate representations of a group. No stereotypes in this rebellion. And what's more, these read-aloud books are written and/or illustrated by people from traditionally marginalized groups.

- Is not a one and done. We are rereaders in this rebellion. Your rebellious read aloud is going to be so loved and referenced, you'll be purchasing additional copies just to make it through a school year. These are stories you'll go back to as your students learn more topics in different content areas to support their thinking.

- Will be a catalyst for a conversation, not the end of it. Your students will be inspired by the read aloud, they'll be ready to engage deeper, and they'll want to take action. Your work isn't finished simply because you closed the pages of the book.

- Does not make you an antiracist. I know this seems harsh, but reading these books and building an inclusive library does not make you an antiracist. It does mean you are being thoughtful and purposeful as you help your students become better citizens. I want to be clear that this work doesn't magically transform you into an antiracist. It can, however, aid you in your journey.

Throughout this book, we will dive a bit deeper into texts that can help your students feel connected to ideas, people, thoughts, and places they may have never known before. We

If you're looking for antiracist and antibias resources, check out any or all of these:

- *Start Here, Start Now: A Guide to Antibias and Antiracist Work in Your School Community* by Liz Kleinrock
- *Stamped From the Beginning* by Ibram X. Kendi
- *We Want to Do More Than Survive* by Bettina Love
- *Pedagogy of the Oppressed* by Paulo Freire
- *Black Lives Matter at School* by Jesse Hagopian
- *Teaching for Black Lives* by Dyan Watson
- *So You Want to Talk About Race?* by Ijeoma Oluo
- *Me and White Supremacy* by Layla L. Saad
- *How the Word Is Passed* by Clint Smith

will activate the activist in each of them and will encourage them to get into "good trouble, necessary trouble," as Representative John Lewis urged.

A note about terms: Language evolves and changes over time, and I have tried to use phrasing and terms that are the most up-to-date and inclusive at the time of writing. I recently found, hands down, the best definition of *diversity* I've ever seen. And as we move along through this book together, getting more comfortable with "inviting conversations about diversity with children's books," as the book's subtitle states as our purpose, please keep in mind that this definition of diversity is the one I'm referencing:

> The concept of diversity encompasses acceptance and respect. It means understanding that each individual is unique, and recognizing our individual differences. These can be along the dimensions of race, ethnicity, gender, sexual orientation, socio-economic status, age, physical abilities, religious beliefs, political beliefs, or other ideologies. It is the exploration of these differences in a safe, positive, and nurturing environment. It is about understanding each other and moving beyond simple tolerance to embracing and celebrating the rich dimensions of diversity contained within each individual. (Rice University, n.d.)

This is the diversity we want to celebrate and explore in our rebellious read alouds—and what we want our classrooms and schools and communities to aspire to.

WHY REBELLIOUS READ ALOUDS?

The work in this book is completely inspired by the efforts and intelligence of Black women. Their tireless and often unrecognized work has shifted my thinking as an educator. Their teaching has awakened me, inspired me, and pushed me to be better and do better.

We often hear of the importance of offering students "mirror, window, and sliding glass door" opportunities. But where does this phrase come from?

Rudine Sims Bishop, who is known as the "mother of multicultural literacy," coined the phrase in the early 1990s while examining children's literature. Bishop expressed the need for children to be able to see their own lives reflected in the stories they read. It is of equal importance, Bishop wrote, for children to have exposure to books that are a window, or a view into a new world or new experience that may be greatly different than their own (Chenoweth, 2019).

In Bishop's (1990) words, "Books are sometimes windows, offering views of worlds that may be real or imagined, familiar or strange" (p. ix). She goes on to state:

> These windows are also sliding glass doors, and readers have only to walk through in imagination to become part of whatever world has been created and recreated by the author. Literature transforms human experience and reflects it back to us, and in that reflection we can see our own lives and experiences as part of the larger human experience. (p. ix)

These mirror, window, and sliding glass door experiences are the foundation of the rebellion. These experiences confirm our lives as important; they say our stories are ones worth being told and listened to (mirrors). They expose us to new worlds; they show us that we aren't the only ones, that there is so much more than we know (windows). And these experiences let us imagine what could be, they give us hope, and they push us to look beyond ourselves and to reimagine something more (sliding glass doors). This is why reading books written about and by people in traditionally marginalized groups is crucial for every student.

But these mirror, window, and sliding glass door experiences cannot be done arbitrarily. The act of integrating diverse texts into our classroom libraries and conversations into our daily routine requires building relationships with our students and understanding their lives and experiences. It means looking at our students and our classroom through a culturally responsive lens. It takes learning, unlearning, and new learning in order to do what's right and best for all students.

The lessons I've learned from Hammond's (2015) book *Culturally Responsive Teaching and The Brain: Promoting Authentic Engagement and Rigor Among Culturally and Linguistically Diverse Students* continue to push me as an educator. Hammond's Ready for Rigor framework sets up a learning environment in which every child has the opportunity to be successful. Integration and interaction with children's books about and written by people from traditionally marginalized groups fits into each part of Hammond's framework:

- Awareness: Know and recognize your own cultural lens.
- Learning partnerships: Help students create a positive mindset.
- Information processing: Help students process new content using methods from oral traditions. (Hello, retelling a read aloud!)
- Community of learners and learning environment: Make room for student voice and advocacy. (Ask students: What stories are missing from our library? What stories do you want to hear/read? Is your story reflected in the books in our library?)

When we begin to truly value and understand the students in our classrooms, we can begin to engage with them academically. Hammond's work encourages us to learn our own culture, reflect and understand our bias, and respect and honor the cultures of the students in our classrooms. And by doing so we can push students' learning beyond the page as we create a world of possibilities for them.

And what about the practice of daily read alouds in general? I am sure it will come as little surprise to a rebel like you, but there is an overwhelming number of academic benefits that result from reading aloud with your students. In fact, Neuman et al.'s (2000) work on reading and literacy shows us that "the single most important activity for building . . . understandings and skills essential for reading success appears to be reading aloud to children" (p. 1). Here are just a few of the benefits that result from daily read alouds:

- Comprehension skills: Some students may struggle with reading independently; read alouds give them a decoding break and allow them to focus on the sequence, main idea, and other story elements as they listen to an engaging story (Gold & Gibson, 2001).

- Vocabulary knowledge: Research shows when young children have various and consistent access and experiences around reading and books, they build a larger vocabulary than students who do not (Kindle, 2009; Newton et al., 2008). And teachers can use read-aloud time to directly teach new words. (Just be careful not to overdo it—we want children to enjoy the story after all.)

- Language development, especially in our youngest learners: An insightful article titled "Reading Aloud to Children: The Evidence," by Duursma et al. (2008) states: "One of the most powerful pieces of shared reading is what happens in the pauses between pages and after the book is closed. The use of 'decontextualised' or non-immediate talk and active engagement has proven to be particularly beneficial for children's language enhancement. Non-immediate talk is talk that goes beyond the information in the text or the illustrations, for example, to make connections to the child's past experiences or to the real world (eg, 'you like ice cream'), or to offer explanations (eg, 'he cried because he was sad')" (p. 556).

- Accessibility of new, complex concepts and higher level language: Children can listen on a higher language level than they can read, so reading aloud makes complex ideas more accessible and exposes children to vocabulary and language patterns that are not part of everyday speech. This, in turn, helps them understand the structure of books when they read independently (Fountas & Pinnell, 1996). It exposes less able readers to the same rich and engaging books that fluent readers read on their own and entices them to become better readers.

And beyond academics, read alouds can help children develop socially, emotionally, and creatively. Read alouds (and the conversations that come with them) help students develop empathy, self-awareness, and interpersonal skills.

I'm sure you didn't need much convincing, but you get the picture, right? Read alouds are not only empowering, they are necessary.

Here are some online resources that offer suggestions for effective read alouds:

- "The Power of Reading Aloud to Your Students," International Literacy Association: https://bit.ly/3BmgKY4

- "Why Every Class Needs Read Alouds," by Laura Varlas: https://bit.ly/31c9KAA

- "What Is Interactive Read-Aloud?" Fountas & Pinnell Literacy blog: https://bit.ly/3EFku9d

WHAT ABOUT LEARNING STANDARDS?

As an educator, I understand the need to constantly connect learning experiences to standards or skills. Standards are our guideposts; they are a part of the job that will never go away. When I started to think about the rebellion and what it means to push ourselves and our students to a new place of learning about the world, my focus shifted to the "what abouts?": those voices (usually from administrators or decision makers) that whisper for assessments, skill-based tests, or learning expectations. The "what abouts?" want the learning objectives posted and changed daily.

The bad news is there's little way to escape the "what abouts?" The good news is that with rebellious read alouds we can conquer them. (And every lesson in this book contains English language arts learning standards connections.)

After reading *Disrupting Thinking* by Beers and Probst (2017), I wanted to be sure our rebellious read alouds went beyond simply a book being read aloud. I wanted to ensure they ignited a discussion to help students understand what we had just read and connect with the story in a meaningful way. Taking what we understand about Bishop's work of mirrors, windows, and sliding glass doors and combining the thoughtful and intentional culturally responsive teaching we learned from Hammond, let's uncover how we can successfully integrate learning standards with developmentally appropriate teaching in the rebellion.

Disrupting Thinking helps educators teach students how to think more critically about the text in front of them. Beers and Probst encourage us to have students make connections in multiple ways. While I found their advice to be incredibly helpful, the book was written with older students in mind. I knew firsthand from working with younger students that this work would require a more developmentally appropriate strategy.

We are familiar with the learning standards that require students to ask and answer questions about key details in a text. Many of us interpret this vague standard to mean "students will be able to discuss and understand what they have read." But how do we teach students to understand and discuss what they have read? How do we scaffold that book talk experience for them in a developmentally appropriate way? Beers and Probst (2017) mention the BHH framework, which represents in the **b**ook, in the **h**ead, in the **h**eart: *In the book* refers to looking at the information directly provided in the book. *In the head* asks readers to think about "what surprised you or what did the author think you knew." *In the heart* asks readers to think about how they emotionally responded to the book.

I took this framework and reworked the connections in a way that made sense for early childhood learners *and* would encourage students to participate in conversations around hushed topics: heart connection, idea connection, and life connection.

Let's begin by thinking of the various ways we make connections to a text.

HEART CONNECTION

You most often have called it a text-to-self connection. This story relates to something in my own life or my own personal experience. Let's call this a *heart connection*. How did this book relate to you personally? Does the character have the same skin color as you? Do the characters live in a similar location as you? Do you know someone with the same name as that character?

For extremely egocentric learners, this is the easiest and most frequent connection to make. It is completely normal for most of your learners to make this connection throughout a rebellious read aloud. Honor their experience and point of view.

IDEA CONNECTION

You may not have used this connection as often when working with young readers. This connection is the spark of something new. The *idea connection* is sparked when a reader learns something brand-new or is inspired by something they've read. An idea connection sounds like this: "Whoa! I did not know people lived there!" "Does everyone eat rice like that?" "Is it OK for boys to wear dresses too?" "What language are they speaking? I've never heard of that!" "I think I may want to try strawberries. That book made them look so yummy!"

Our students often think about these connections in their head but don't have the opportunity to voice them. Many students have been trained to keep their rebellious thoughts in their heads for fear of offending someone. By encouraging these conversations, we are encouraging curiosity and eliminating negative bias and stereotypes. It is imperative to give young children the opportunity to voice their idea connections out loud and spend considerable time uncovering their understanding.

As educators, this may be a time when you feel vulnerable. Don't be afraid to say, "I don't know. Let's look it up!" or "I used to think that too, but then I read about ____ and I changed my thinking!" Show your students the power in not knowing and unlearning. How rebellious of you!

LIFE CONNECTION

This is the vaguest of connections, and that's on purpose. It's an opportunity for young learners to make connections that are meaningful to them on their own terms. It could be a connection to something they've read before. It could be a connection to something they know is happening in the world but really don't have the context to process properly. It gives our young readers the chance to feel like their connections and voice are valid no matter what.

So what does that look like in the classroom and how can you be sure you're touching on the learning standards? While I wholeheartedly believe that not all learning needs to be documented in a worksheet/exit ticket/quiz, I understand the realities of teaching. One way that helped me pair these important conversations with teaching expectations was to allow my students to journal their response to the read aloud. Of course, this develops after repeated modeled lessons and slowly scaffolded lessons, but yes, five-year-old students in my classroom are able to journal their response to our daily read aloud and document the ways they connected to the story.

Here's how I do it: After explaining the different ways to connect to a story (with visual and American Sign Language references), I chart each student's connection response. (Visit the book's online companion, resources.corwin.com/rebellious, to view a video of this conversation.) That one step is enough for the first day. This initial step allows everyone to see how others have connected to the story. It shows students there is never a wrong way to make a connection to a story as long as you can explain your connection.

The next day, we revisit parts of the story (remember, a read aloud doesn't have to be a one and done). We revisit our chart, and I give students the opportunity to change their connections if needed.

Name: _____

I want to grow strawberries

Our next step is to make the abstract concrete. Pull out exactly why students are connecting to stories. Give them an opportunity to share their own stories, be vulnerable about what they don't know, and ask curious questions. During this part of the lesson, I provide students with a journal page to record their responses (see image; a downloadable is available at resources.corwin .com/rebellious). They color in the type of connection they made (heart, chain, or lightbulb) and then draw and write (if ready) the way they have connected to that particular story.

The first time a student journals their connection, be sure to validate their response. There really isn't a wrong way to connect to a story. Just be sure students are matching their connection to the correct way to connect (i.e., new idea to the lightbulb icon). Additionally, give students visuals and vocabulary to allow them to accurately retell their connection. Scaffolding this experience early on will create a strong foundation for powerful and impactful conversations later.

The image to the left shows how a student responded to the text *We Are Grateful* by Traci Sorell. (Find a downloadable connection page at **resources.corwin.com/ rebellious**.)

This child's response is a great example of how students make connections to a story that features a culture different from their own. Opportunities to talk with students about what they notice and how they connect or question what they've learned allow them to develop into the global learners we want them to be.

These journal entries do not have to come after every rebellious read aloud. But the entries do provide a nice opportunity to check the progress of your students' connections to the read alouds. They also serve as a way to take care of the "have tos" we all must deal with as educators. One of the biggest takeaways from these activities (and the accompanying conversations) is just how ready students are to make connections with the world around them.

Taking all we know from Bishop, Hammond, and Beers and Probst, and by considering all the research-backed benefits of read alouds in general, we understand the foundations of the rebellion. By creating mirror, window, and sliding glass door opportunities, we are helping every student feel valued, seen, and respected. By thinking critically about our own culture and bias, we ensure every student feels safe taking chances in their learning in our classrooms. By encouraging students to think critically about the connections they make while reading, we quiet the "what abouts?" and engage our learners in necessary and important conversations. We begin to push back on the traditional ways we've been asked to engage with students around books. We encourage students to find themselves in the learning, in the conversation, in the story.

In Part 2 of this book, I walk you through lessons that can guide conversations around specific books. These will serve as a scaffold until you're comfortable planning, teaching, and discussing rebellious read alouds on your own. The lessons are organized around curricular themes that appear in most elementary classrooms. And every lesson is formed around Literacy Learning Standards from the Common Core State Standards (you can adapt these according to the standards your school follows). I've also included connections to the Learning for Justice (2021) Social Justice Standards to indicate the importance of the work from a social action stance. Keep in mind these words from the Learning for Justice website:

> The Social Justice Standards are a road map for anti-bias education at every stage of K–12 instruction. Comprised of anchor standards and age-appropriate learning outcomes, the Standards provide a common language and organizational structure educators can use to guide curriculum development and make schools more just and equitable. (para. 1)

Access the complete Social Justice Standards online here:

https://www.learningforjustice.org/frameworks/social-justice-standards

I have used these standards as part of my planning practice for the last six years of teaching. Not only are they developmentally appropriate, but they also include scenarios for educators to build a concrete understanding of what to expect each standard to look like in the classroom. You can find the complete standards for each domain (identity, diversity, action, justice) on the Learning for Justice website. You'll find every specific domain has been included throughout the read-aloud lesson plans; the Appendix also includes an at-a-glance chart that shows book titles alphabetically along with their Social Justice Standards and Literacy Learning Standards.

The Learning for Justice Social Justice Standards encourage educators to dig deeper into the social studies elements we know are important for young children. It's not enough for us to say "be nice," for example; we must help our students have a concrete understanding of what "niceness" looks like in various scenarios as they interact with different people. Not only will you find the standards helpful, there are also in-depth lessons for educators—lessons for each domain strand that help you develop a stronger understanding of what you'll be helping students unpack using the standards. Pretty helpful, right?

HOW DO I CULTIVATE A DIVERSE CLASSROOM LIBRARY?

Remember that definition of diversity from earlier? What strikes me, particularly, are the final two sentences: "It is the exploration of these differences in a safe, positive, and nurturing environment. It is about understanding each other and moving beyond simple tolerance to embracing and celebrating the rich dimensions of diversity contained within each individual." I started to think: How can I make my classroom a space where students can explore diversity safely in a positive and nurturing environment? They need to see themselves (mirrors), they need to see their classmates (windows), and they need opportunities to consider varying perspectives and viewpoints (sliding glass doors). What better entry point than our daily read-aloud sessions?

I took a long hard look at my classroom library. I spent an entire summer reorganizing it. I sorted books by topic, which allowed me to see the varying numbers of books in our library. We had a ton of books with animal characters but very few books about historical events. We had a lot of books about ocean animals but few books on different types of foods. This wasn't bad or wrong. It just meant that there were limited types of stories being shared in our library. Our library wasn't inclusive of multiple experiences, points of view, languages, or ways of thinking.

If you're looking for a great way to survey the diversity and inclusiveness of your own library, please check out Lee and Low's classroom questionnaire:

https://bit.ly/3mB0C0J

Next, I needed to consider the students in my classroom. What was their first language, who lived with them at home, what were their interests, what types of things did they talk about during snack/recess/lunch? I had to understand what books they wanted to read instead of what books I wanted them to read. Not every Black student wants to read books only about the American Black experience. Children are not monoliths. They have varied life experiences and interests. I had to talk to my students about our library and how we could make it a place they wanted to experience and enjoy reading.

One way to do this was to have a book interview with each student. This doesn't have to happen all at once and should happen multiple times throughout the year. It's a great way to assess how children see themselves as readers and how your classroom library is helping them build a positive identity as a reader. I include the following questions in the interview:

- Do the characters in the books in our library resemble you?

- Are there stories in our library that are similar to stories in your life?

- Do you see characters in our books who are different from you?

- Are there stories in our library that you are interested in reading?

- What's one thing we can do to make our library better?

(You can access a printable version of the interview from the book's companion website, resources.corwin.com/rebellious.)

The next step is probably the most tedious, expensive, and time-consuming: finding the right books.

THIS TAKES RESEARCH

When you're looking at books that share a particular perspective, be sure to find books that are written by "own voices" authors and illustrators. The hashtag #ownvoices was started by author Corinne Duyvis. These are books that are written and/or illustrated by people who have experienced a similar story or situation as in the book. For example, a story about experiencing racism in the United States should be written by a person of color in order to get an accurate perspective on that story. Similarly, a story about the experience of an Indigenous person should be written by an Indigenous person.

THIS TAKES THRIFTINESS

I know firsthand how expensive it can be to purchase items for your classroom, especially children's books. However, there are several resources to help you get books at a deep discount or, better yet, for free!

- Visit your local secondhand or thrift stores. There are used bookstores online, too.

- Don't forget about your local public library! There are books in the library just waiting to aid you in your rebellious journey. If they don't have a copy, just ask. They'll be happy to order a book for you!

- If you teach at a Title 1 school, the website firstbook.org offers recently published books at a deep discount.

- Depending on your location, you may be able to receive donated books from Half Price Books (www.hpb.com). Half Price Books also offers an educator discount for purchases.

- If your district/school allows you to use DonorsChoose, then do so repeatedly. Most of our classroom library has been built due to projects from DonorsChoose being fulfilled.

- Consider creating a wish list on your favorite online or local bookstore that's easily accessible to others—and share it broadly.

- Does your campus have a PTA or Parent/Caregiver Organization? Share your rebellious list with them, and encourage them to purchase books for home reading or the school's library.

Don't feel as if you have to rush to pack your library full of great books overnight. Cultivating an inclusive library takes time if it's done purposefully and thoughtfully.

Here are some resources to use in order to ensure the books you find tell an accurate story:

- Follow Debbie Reese on social media (@debreese) or check her website for more in-depth information: https://americanindiansinchildrensliterature.blogspot.com/

- Follow @WeNeedDiverseBooks and its hashtag, #weneeddiversebooks, on social media.

- If you're looking for a librarian's perspective on great books, check out Mike over at @thebookwrangler on Instagram.

- I use my own social media accounts to share upcoming diverse titles. You can find me at @thetututeacher or @diversereads.

Hopefully, the titles recommended in this book can provide a starting place for you as you begin your journey.

Once you have the books, then what? Having a diverse collection of books is crucial, but it is only the first step. How you engage your students in thoughtful conversations around these texts is vital. Using texts to help students understand the world around them (and worlds far away) is the beginning of the rebellion.

ARE YOUNG PEOPLE DEVELOPMENTALLY READY FOR THESE CONVERSATIONS?

But Vera, you ask, are young people *really* ready to have these conversations around hushed topics?

Yes.

The infographic created by the Children's Community School—"They're not too young to talk about race!"—uses research-based findings to indicate the developmental readiness of young children to have conversations around race. You'll notice that by five years old, children begin to show similar racial attitudes as adults. Young children are learning to think about race based on what we are or aren't talking to them about. The conversations we choose not to have, and the moments we quiet their curiosity only further solidify their understanding (or lack of understanding) about the people around them.

If we accept these findings about race to be true, then we can assume the findings would be similar for other areas of our identity, such as gender, religion, class, disability, and more. What we are called to do as early childhood educators is create a space that inspires and encourages young children to ask curious questions that help them make sense of themselves and the world around them.

If a teachable moment shows itself—whether around race, gender, friendship, emotions, or another topic—stop and address it. To not address it is to either allow a misconception to become a reality or not allow the victim to have a voice. And I will be honest—with the 301,234,273 things teachers juggle all day long, it can be difficult to find the time to stop and address every issue. But if I don't, and the next teacher doesn't, and the next one and the next one, misconceptions start to become reality, and as we all know, that can be incredibly harmful.

I want to be clear that books are just one way to start a rebellious conversation. Picture books offer entry points to thinking and talking, and read alouds are a tried-and-true instructional and social-emotional fixture in most elementary classrooms. When considering integrating these titles into our classrooms, I thought of all the ways in which teachers are working through the things we "must" teach and things we know we should spend more time teaching. The pressures of teaching regional or state standards can make purposeful integration feel overwhelming. The idea of looking at a task in small or "bite-sized" portions isn't new. However, utilizing this approach when considering rebellious conversations can make the rebellion seem possible. Small steps toward change. The structure discussed after the infographic shows one way to consider approaching these rebellious conversations through read alouds.

They're not too young to talk about race!

0	1	2	3	4	5	6+

0: At birth, babies look equally at faces of all races. At 3 months, babies look more at faces that match the race of their caregivers. (Kelly et al. 2005)

1: Children as young as two years use race to reason about people's behaviors. (Hirschfeld, 2008)

2: By 30 months, most children use race to choose playmates. (Katz & Kofkin, 1997)

3: Expressions of racial prejudice often peak at ages 4 and 5. (Aboud, 2008)

4: By five, Black and Latinx children in research settings show no preference toward their own groups compared to Whites; White children at this age remain strongly biased in favor of whiteness. (Dunham et al. 2008)

5: By kindergarten, children show many of the same racial attitudes that adults in our culture hold—they have already learned to associate some groups with higher status than others. (Kinzler, 2016)

6+: Explicit conversations with 5–7 year olds about interracial friendship can dramatically improve their racial attitudes in as little as a single week. (Bronson & Merryman, 2009)

Young children notice and think about race. Adults often worry that talking about race will encourage racial bias in children, but the opposite is true. **Silence about race reinforces racism** by letting children draw their own conclusions based on what they see. Teachers and families can play a powerful role in helping children of all ages develop positive attitudes about race and diversity and skills to promote a more just future—but only if we talk about it!

Do some learning of your own to get ready for conversations with children. Here are some good places to seek *information* and *training*:

- Teaching Tolerance — tolerance.org
- Raising Race Conscious Children — raceconscious.org
- Embrace Race — embracerace.org
- Teaching for Change — teachingforchange.org
- AORTA Cooperative — aorta.coop
- Fortify Community Health (CA) — fortifycommunityhealth@gmail.com
- Delaware Valley Assoc. for the Education of Young Children (PA) — dvaeyc.org

START SMALL

These are the must-haves. This is like dipping your toes in the water to see how cold it is. The small allows for all students to connect to the story in a way that makes sense for them.

BE CONSISTENT

Consistency is key. This part of the lesson will invite students to think a bit deeper about the ways in which the story highlights similarities or differences between their own experiences and those of the characters. These are the "zoom in" moments that allow you to revisit a text multiple times.

KEEP CONSTANT

Reading books and having conversations are great. But how do we help our young learners take action? How do we help them become allies and co-conspirators? How do we help them unlearn harmful bias/stereotypes/ideas and become critical, conscious changemakers?

Start small. Be consistent. Keep constant. This is the framework that organizes all the lessons in this book. Does this framework feel reasonable? I hope it's reasonable, but I also hope there's a bit of a challenge for you. That challenge will push you to continue to ask your students important questions.

When you sit with your students, book in hand, ready to engage in rebellious conversations, you'll do a lot of the talking at first. Just like with any other lesson, you are going to model some of the questioning and the out-loud thinking you want your students to do. For example:

> "Wow. It makes me feel really sad and angry that the character's granddad wasn't allowed to vote especially after waiting for so long to have the legal right to vote. I'm wondering if there's anything happening in our world today that prevents people from accessing their right to vote. Let's do some research!"

> "I noticed that the illustrator drew a sad face on Aiden's mirror. Why do you think they included that in the picture? How do you think that helps us understand how someone who is transgender might feel? Does this sad face stay for the rest of the book? Let's read to find out more."

The simple pauses, the words we focus on, the questions we ask all help our students start to make sense of the world around them. A world they may be unfamiliar with but want to know about.

Further, because all the lessons here can help meet specific language and literacy learning standards, you can meet all those "what abouts?" too.

Are you starting to think to yourself, "OK, I can do this"?

You are? Good. You're ready.

You rebel.

PART Two

Rebellious
Read-Aloud Lessons

HERE WE GO!

There are forty-five lessons in this section. Originally, there were thirty-six, enough to allow for one rebellious read per school-year week. But then I realized, what if the conversations from one book inspire a class to keep the learning going? I can't leave these teachers and students hanging! So I added one more book per theme. This way, if you want to keep the conversation going, you can give your students exactly what they need.

The diagram on the next spread shows all the elements of a rebellious read aloud to guide you through the lessons. As mentioned in Part 1, all lessons contain skills necessary to meet key learning standards as well as social justice standards.

Lessons are organized around themes that appear throughout typical elementary classroom units—names, features, traditions, actions, families, identities, disabilities, foods, and histories—so you can map these read-aloud experiences across your existing curriculum.

At the end of each theme, you'll find an interview with an educator or a parent/caregiver. These "Teacher Talk" interviews provide a bit of insight into how others see the importance and necessity of these conversations. I learned so much from talking with all of the interviewees, and I truly feel that they add a new depth to the experience of the rebellion. We get to hear their stories, learn from their mistakes, and feel encouraged.

Remember, each lesson is a guide. It isn't written in stone, and you don't have to follow it exactly. I want you to make changes that make sense for your students.

A rebel wouldn't stay on the path they were told to walk on, anyway. They'd find the path that was calling them.

Learning for Justice
Social Justice Standards

These are those important elements that help students think about how social justice is interwoven into all parts of our lives and experiences. Be sure to check out the Learning for Justice website for a more detailed explanation of their standards (www.learningforjustice.org/frameworks/social-justice-standards).

ELA Standards

These are the skill elements we must build into instruction. Each lesson provides the Common Core State Standards Reading: Literature Standards for Grade 1. (I used first grade as a guiding point for standards; adapt these standards to whatever standards your school requires.)

Book Biography

I've provided a quick synopsis of each book. You can choose to read this to your students before you dig into the text or use it for yourself to gauge whether this is the book for you.

Vera's View

This is one of my favorite parts of each lesson. It tells you what each book means to me. It gives a quick and personal insight into how each of these titles really does give us (the readers) an opportunity to connect, to learn, to change our minds, and to expand our horizons.

Start Small

These are the questions you most likely are already asking your students. There isn't anything wrong with these questions, so don't feel like they are too easy or basic or not getting at the "meat" of the book. These are stepping stones. They allow your students to find a personal connection to the story (and that's what we want!).

OUR NAMES ARE IMPORTANT

These lessons feature books that share the ways we can celebrate and honor the names of the students in our classrooms. From pronunciation to chosen names, students will be invited to engage in conversations around the importance of names.

ALMA AND HOW SHE GOT HER NAME
Written and illustrated by Juana Martinez-Neal

LEARNING FOR JUSTICE STANDARDS
Identity
Diversity

ELA STANDARDS
- Students will ask and answer questions about key details in a text.
- Students will acknowledge differences in the points of view of characters.
- Students will describe how characters in a story respond to major events and challenges.

BOOK BIOGRAPHY

Alma's name is much too long. It barely fits on a page when it's written out. Alma starts to wonder just how she managed to get such a big name! Will Alma learn how to love her name?

VERA'S VIEW

My full name is composed of five different names. Each name has a special history and story of its own. Where I grew up, many people had multiple names, so I always felt like my name was long enough, just like my friends. Names have so much power and can tell a story all on their own.

START SMALL
Opening pages (double spread)

How long is your name? How many words are in your name? How many letters are in your name?

20 ● Rebellious Read Alouds

OUR NAMES ARE IMPORTANT

BE CONSISTENT

The world is so big… (double spread)

Alma has marked the different places her ancestors are from. How does knowing where her ancestors are from make her name more special?

José was my father… (double spread)

Part of Alma's name comes from her grandfather's name. Do names belong to only one gender?

KEEP CONSTANT

The history of someone's name can be tricky. Some people have names that they might not know the history of. Some people have names that don't make sense for who they truly are. What is most important is that we honor and respect someone's name.

LET'S MAKE A PLAN OF ACTION

- How can we be sensitive to knowing the history of people's names?
- How does your name tell your story?
- Why is it important to take the time to learn and understand the story of someone's name? How do you take time to learn more about others by understanding their name and their history?

Because I read this book, I now know _____ .

Because I read this book, I wonder _____ .

Because I read this book, I understand _____ .

Our Names Are Important ● 21

Be Consistent

These are the questions we should always be asking: Who's voice is missing? Why is that voice missing? What am I unlearning? How have my biases prevented me from fully understanding someone else's point of view? These questions may encourage you to confront your own biases in order to be able to invite and encourage these rebellious conversations with your students.

Keep Constant

In this section, we examine *why* these questions, these books, this rebellion is important. This section can be for you, for your students, or it can even be added to your classroom newsletter for caregivers to access.

Let's Make a Plan of Action

These questions move your students from discussion to actual action. We want our students to do more than just enjoy a rebellious read aloud; we want them to feel emboldened to make a change—a change for themselves and a change for others. This section is expansive; it's a place to start and keep moving.

Because I Read This Book

When I added this section, I added it with the students in mind. But as I worked through the different lessons, I thought that it might be helpful for educators to use this as a note-taking section for themselves and provide an entry point for students—for example, "You know, class, when I first read this book, I didn't know that people celebrated this holiday and that there are so many similarities to this holiday and the traditions my family celebrates. So now that I read this book, I know that Eid is a time of reflection and community."

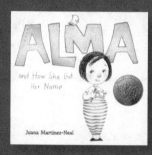

LEARNING FOR JUSTICE STANDARDS

Identity
Diversity

ELA STANDARDS

- Students will ask and answer questions about key details in a text.

- Students will acknowledge differences in the points of view of characters.

- Students will describe how characters in a story respond to major events and challenges.

These lessons feature books that share the ways we can celebrate and honor the names of the students in our classrooms. From pronunciation to chosen names, students will be invited to engage in conversations around the importance of names.

ALMA AND HOW SHE GOT HER NAME

Written and illustrated by Juana Martinez-Neal

BOOK BIOGRAPHY

Alma's name is much too long. It barely fits on a page when it's written out. Alma starts to wonder just how she managed to get such a big name! Will Alma learn how to love her name?

VERA'S VIEW

My full name is composed of five different names. Each name has a special history and story of its own. Where I grew up, many people had multiple names, so I always felt like my name was long enough, just like my friends. Names have so much power and can tell a story all on their own.

START SMALL

Opening pages (double spread)

How long is your name? How many words are in your name? How many letters are in your name?

BE CONSISTENT

The world is so big…(double spread)

Alma has marked the different places her ancestors are from. How does knowing where her ancestors are from make her name more special?

José was my father…(double spread)

Part of Alma's name comes from her grandfather's name. Do names belong to only one gender?

KEEP CONSTANT

The history of someone's name can be tricky. Some people have names that they might not know the history of. Some people have names that don't make sense for who they truly are. What is most important is that we honor and respect someone's name.

LET'S MAKE A PLAN OF ACTION

- How can we be sensitive to knowing the history of people's names?
- How does your name tell your story?
- Why is it important to take the time to learn and understand the story of someone's name? How do you take time to learn more about others by understanding their name and their history?

Because I read this book, I now know _____ .

Because I read this book, I wonder _____ .

Because I read this book, I understand _____ .

LEARNING FOR JUSTICE STANDARDS

Identity
Diversity
Justice
Action

ELA STANDARDS

- Students will ask and answer questions about key details in a text.

- Students will acknowledge differences in the points of view of characters.

- Students will describe how characters in a story respond to major events and challenges.

ALWAYS ANJALI

Written by Sheetal Sheth
Illustrated by Jessica Blank

BOOK BIOGRAPHY

Anjali wants nothing more for her birthday than a new bicycle! On the morning of her birthday, her parents surprise her with a brand-new bicycle. Anjali and her friends visit a fair, where they find a stand that sells bike license plates with different names featured. Anjali's friends find license plates with their names, but Anjali can't find hers. Later, a boy teases Anjali about her name. Can Anjali learn to love her name?

VERA'S VIEW

This is one of my favorite books to use at the beginning of the school year. The illustrations are bright and colorful, and the story is engaging. I print out the students' names in a rectangle, and we create and decorate our own license plates. These are hung up in the classroom all year long.

START SMALL

Opening pages (double spread)

What is one thing you would wish for for your birthday?

BE CONSISTENT

Anjali asked if they had any more plates…(double spread)

How do you think Anjali feels at this moment? Has there ever been a time when you weren't included or represented? How did you feel?

Then she heard laughter…(double spread)

Anjali was being made fun of for her name. Some of the children in the photo look upset; others are laughing. What would you do if you were there? Why is it important to speak up when you see someone being made fun of?

KEEP CONSTANT

Sometimes names can feel hard to pronounce because they are different from names we often hear. That doesn't make the names weird or wrong; it means we have to make a small effort to learn how to pronounce them correctly. If you find a name difficult to pronounce, do not ask if it's OK to call that person by a nickname instead. Honor their name as it is.

LET'S MAKE A PLAN OF ACTION

- What are some words we can say or actions we can take when we see or hear someone being made fun of?
- How do we check in with someone after they've been made fun of?
- What is your school's plan for handling bullies? How can they take accountability and repair the harm they've caused?

Because I read this book, I now know _____ .

Because I read this book, I wonder _____ .

Because I read this book, I understand _____ .

LEARNING FOR JUSTICE STANDARDS

Identity
Diversity
Justice
Action

ELA STANDARDS

- Students will ask and answer questions about key details in a text.

- Students will acknowledge differences in the points of view of characters.

- Students will describe how characters in a story respond to major events and challenges.

► CALL ME MAX

Written by Kyle Lukoff
Illustrated by Luciano Lozano

BOOK BIOGRAPHY

Max is excited but a bit nervous to start school. Max is a boy, but how can Max be sure the students and teachers at school know that? He wants to be called by his name, Max, not the name on his admission papers. How can Max find a way to let his family and friends know this is his true self?

VERA'S VIEW

We often frame the conversation around the importance of names by focusing on pronunciation. Equally important is acknowledging the name our students would like to be called. Encouraging children to advocate for themselves and correct someone when they use their incorrect name is an important lesson.

START SMALL

Opening pages (double spread)

What do you see when you look in the mirror? What are the features you notice when you look in the mirror? What is your favorite feature?

BE CONSISTENT

Transgender is a long word…(double spread)

Have you heard the word *transgender* before? The author tells us that "when a baby grows up to be transgender, it means that the grown up who said they were a boy or a girl made a mistake."

But school turned out to be hard…(double spread)

Can you think of some ways school is hard for you? How do you think school is hard for Max? What are some ways the school can support Max?

Can you call me Max? (double spread)

Why do you think Max doesn't want us to know his old name? Why is that something that would be important to someone who is transgender?

I decided to hold it all day…(page)

Is it safe for Max to not go to the restroom at school all day? Is it safe for Max to not drink water all day? What are some things the school could do to make using the restroom safer for Max? Does your school have a bathroom that is safe for everyone?

KEEP CONSTANT

Call Me Max has been called a "controversial" book. Many schools and districts have banned the book due to the character being transgender. What are ways your school or district supports transgender students? How can you help educate families and students about the importance of keeping transgender students safe at school?

LET'S MAKE A PLAN OF ACTION

Max's family are still figuring out how to be the best family for Max. They aren't afraid to ask questions and ask for help when they don't understand something.

- Who do you ask for help when you don't understand?
- How do you become someone that other people can ask for help?
- What can you do if you make a mistake by misgendering someone?

Because I read this book, I now know _____ .

Because I read this book, I wonder _____ .

Because I read this book, I understand _____ .

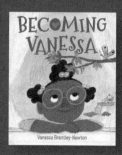

LEARNING FOR JUSTICE STANDARDS

Identity
Diversity
Justice
Action

ELA STANDARDS

- Students will ask and answer questions about key details in a text.

- Students will acknowledge differences in the points of view of characters.

- Students will describe how characters in a story respond to major events and challenges.

BECOMING VANESSA

Written and illustrated by Vanessa Brantley-Newton

BOOK BIOGRAPHY

Becoming Vanessa celebrates the beauty of being unique. Just like a caterpillar, Vanessa undergoes a metamorphosis. By the end of the story, she realizes that being exactly who she is is the best way to show others just how special she is.

VERA'S VIEW

When I was a young girl, I didn't like my name. I thought it was so foreign as I had never met a child who had a name similar to mine. I thought my name was "too much" and vowed to change it when I was an adult. It wasn't until my mother told me the meaning behind my name (it comes from the Latin word *veritas*, meaning truth) that I embraced the beauty of my own name.

START SMALL

Opening pages (double spread)

How did you feel on the first day of school? Were you worried other students wouldn't like you?

BE CONSISTENT

Next everyone wrote their names…(double spread)

It is taking Vanessa a little longer than the other students to write her name. Why do you think it takes more time for her? Does it matter that it takes her a bit longer than everyone else? Why or why not? Are there some things you can do quickly? Are there some things it takes you a little longer to do? Why do you think that is?

Do you know why I named you…(double spread)

What is your name? What is your favorite thing about your name?

KEEP CONSTANT

There are many ways people express themselves. Think of all the different ways you have seen people express themselves. Do they wear bright and colorful clothing? Do they move their bodies in a certain way? Do they sing songs? Do they write poems or stories?

How can we support people in the way they choose to express themselves? How can learning about the different ways of self-expression help us become kinder people?

LET'S MAKE A PLAN OF ACTION

It's important to talk about your feelings.

It is OK to feel all kinds of feelings.

- Have you ever felt upset about something?
- Did you ever feel like pushing your feelings away?
- Who is someone you talk to when you want to talk about your feelings?
- How can you be someone that others can come talk to about their feelings?

Because I read this book, I now know _____ .

Because I read this book, I wonder _____ .

Because I read this book, I understand _____ .

OUR NAMES ARE IMPORTANT

LEARNING FOR JUSTICE STANDARDS

Identity
Diversity
Justice
Action

ELA STANDARDS

- Students will ask and answer questions about key details in a text.

- Students will acknowledge differences in the points of view of characters.

- Students will describe how characters in a story respond to major events and challenges.

YOUR NAME IS A SONG

Written by Jamilah Thompkins-Bigelow
Illustrated by Luisa Uribe

BOOK BIOGRAPHY

Kora-Jalimuso was gifted a beautiful name. Her teacher has trouble pronouncing her name correctly. After her first day of school, Kora is frustrated with the way her teacher and the other students incorrectly say her name. A chat with her mother reminds Kora that her name is like a song and that all names are important and are deserving of respect. The next day, Kora sings her teacher's name and other children's names, showing them the beauty in their names. Finally, Kora sings her name proudly and loudly for everyone to hear and sing (correctly) along.

VERA'S VIEW

As someone whose name is constantly pronounced incorrectly, marbled out of mouths as if my mother didn't spend days cultivating my name to describe the essence of who I am, I remember hating my name. It was so different from everyone else's name. And I never knew a Vera who was my own age. It wasn't until I was older that I began to fall in love with my name. Carved from the Latin word *veritas*, my name means truth.

I love this book. I love this book. Every classroom needs this book for the beginning of the year. Our names are important; they are gifts from our family. Every name is a song.

START SMALL

Opening pages (double spread)

What do you think Kora is thinking at this moment?

Why do you think that? Why isn't she playing with the other students?

BE CONSISTENT

At the red light…(page)

Where do you think the characters live? Is it a city, a suburb, is it out in the country? Why is the location important to this story? Does the location change what we think about the character?

Momma pointed up…(page)

Why is it important that the mom says, "Their real names were stolen long ago"?

Do you have an idea what time in history she could be referring to?

Why is this important for a Black family to talk about?

Did you notice the name Trayvon written in the sky? Visit the glossary in the back of the book to find out who Trayvon was.

Why do you think the author decided to include Trayvon's name?

What are other ways we honor someone?

KEEP CONSTANT

Learning new names can be overwhelming, especially if we aren't familiar with the correct way to pronounce them.

LET'S MAKE A PLAN OF ACTION

- What can we say when we say someone's name wrong?
- How can we learn how to say their name correctly?
- What do we do if we hear someone mispronounce someone's name?

Because I read this book, I now know _____ .

Because I read this book, I wonder _____ .

Because I read this book, I understand _____ .

TEACHER TALK

FEATURED EDUCATOR: Juan Edgar Gonzales Jr.

Houston, Texas. Third grade. Twelve years in the elementary classroom. BIPOC educator—the global majority. Pronouns: he/him. (View this video interview on the companion website, resources.corwin.com/rebellious.)

VERA: Can you talk to me a bit about your experience with teaching "controversial" topics through read alouds?

JUAN: I think when you get to be an educator and you realize that you can use this platform to share stories, it's a journey. In the beginning, it's just fun and it's exciting. And then you realize that there's so much that you can do with it. It's more than just sharing a story. And I remember in the beginning, when I started realizing that being able to share stories wasn't necessarily just for content, it was this ability to share real-life stories and expose students to the world. I remember in the beginning, I was timid and like, "Can I share stories of race? Can I share stories of backgrounds that are different from than what I know my students are growing up in?" And for a small chunk of time, I remember I would even send home letters, just so I could, not clear my name, but let parents know what was going on in the classroom.

And just say, "I share stories from all different backgrounds. And if you want to have conversations about what this is." And I remember the reason I don't do that anymore is because I remember my brother, who is gay, he saw the letter and asked me, "Am I controversial? Who I decide to love." And my letter said something like, the stories that I'm sharing could be considered controversial nature. Right? And then all of a sudden I realized that I was labeling this group of people as something that is something bad to talk about, when really they're just part of our world. And so when my brother opened my eyes to that, I'd realized even when I was trying to do good, and this is all a learning journey, right? I'm not ashamed to talk about this. I was still doing harm.

And so for me, now it's more like, of course that comes with my own privilege of knowing the admin that I work under, confidence from teaching. The longer you teach, you have more confidence to say, "When I share literacy, I know this is my chance to show students the world." And so now it's no longer about getting people ready or making them aware of what this could be, it's just knowing that the stories that I share, when there are good stories to share, regardless of what those backgrounds are, it doesn't matter, it's about good stories and making sure that students see stories from all different backgrounds. So now I'm at a place with it where it's not so scary, but the journey there wasn't as easy as I'm just going to do it.

VERA: What are some challenges you've faced?

JUAN: Yeah. I've had experiences with both admin and parents. When I say, like, "I want to show students the world," it's not about imposing ideas on them. It's about showing them that other things exist outside of you. One of the things about me being as an educator and not a perfect life, but I lived a good life, like I had the privilege of having a really great life. And one of the biggest things that I learned being an educator is realizing, wow, kids don't get to grow up the same way. I was so conditioned to thinking everybody's childhood was [like mine]. That's how privileged I was, and I didn't realize how different everybody is and so that's why I think read aloud is so important because we get to show them that there's a world that exists outside of you. And for me, that's why it's important to be a rebellious reader, to not sticking to the norms and show students these stories.

And so when you do these things, admin and parents will think that you're imposing ideas and that's not what this is. This is exposure. This is to build compassion and understanding, so that in the moment that you go out into the real world and you meet these people that have different backgrounds, you have something to leverage with, to understand, to build a connection with and not just feel like they're outside of the norm. One time I had a parent who saw the stories that I was sharing on social media (because I also have the privilege of getting to talk to other educators and show educators what I'm reading in the classroom). And that parent saw the author of one of the books that I was sharing and did research on the author and somehow connected that the author's ideas were my ideas, and those were the ideas that I was using in the classroom.

And so, this is why communication is so important because it's parents and all of us have to have [communicate that] it's never about imposing ideas and you can't just see something and think and create your own narrative with it because you're nervous about something that feels different; that is not normal. You think it can impact your child in a different way. I think as educators, we have to have that communication open to parents and administration to understand why we do this, why we want to have these read alouds that are considered rebellious, but really it's not anything about imposing. And so that was the big conversation, a big heartfelt conversation I remember that I had with this parent, where I talked to them through the whole night because while in the beginning, even I felt like I was being accused of something that wasn't true.

Ultimately I understood this was a misunderstanding. Like them finding a way to kind of have this communication with me and going about it the wrong way. And then having to have a really big conversation about why I do the things I do in the classroom, and why their student is better for it. And so I think as educators, we have to make sure that we communicate not in a way that we are labeling these stories that we're reading as something that's controversial, but just why we do it, why it's important. And if it's not something that you're used to, here's why you should also consider it to be part of your home life and not just in school.

VERA: Why is the work of integrating rebellious books into your daily read-aloud schedule important or meaningful to you?

JUAN: Like I said earlier, I don't want the students that I get to work with, I don't want them to grow up and one day be like, wow, why didn't anyone tell me about this? And I think one of the biggest struggles I've had in my adult life, and even as an educator, is realizing things and learning things and saying, why didn't anyone tell me this? Like, where was this conversation? Why didn't anyone show me this? And I feel like when you have more knowledge, when you understand people, when you know different backgrounds, do you feel more connected to the world? You feel more hungry for more knowledge. And so giving students these opportunities is really just to me what literacy is all about, regardless of what the stories you're sharing, it's an opportunity for a better life. And being able to understand who they are and understanding the world that they exist in better. And when you have that understanding, you get to walk through life a little bit more confident, a little bit more connected. And I want to give that to the students that I work with. And so that's why it's important to me.

VERA: Mm-hmm [affirmative]. 100%. I think it also brings a bit of excitement. It's exciting to know that people behave this way, somewhere far away, or that kids go to school on boats or whatever we might learn or find out. That's exciting. And it inspires curiosity. And I feel like, why not? Why wouldn't you want to have a classroom full of confident and curious children?

JUAN: 1000% I totally agree. And I think those are like the real learning moments. Those moments where somebody tells you something and you're like, really? This happens or this exists? And so providing so many different types of stories creates opportunities for those moments. And yeah, you're so right, it's exciting.

VERA: What have you noticed in your students/children as a result of rebellious read alouds?

JUAN: The work of an educator is hard. And I always say, one of the biggest things that will always keep me in this line of work is the stories that I get to share with students. Because when we teach reading, of course there's a side to it that's academic, but really, just the big bulk of teaching readers is life. I always say teaching reading is teaching life, and getting to have these conversations. And so for me, when I share stories about students that can identify because they've never seen their culture or their country that they're from represented in a book, and how that initiates this excitement to say, well, I need to find more authors that also write this way or more stories that look like me. To me, that's the biggest part of representation that's so exciting. Or seeing not just culture, but also seeing two dads, two moms—that's something that I've had the experience with.

I remember a young girl that I worked with when I was reading stories about women and women's history month, and that inspired her so much to want to go and do the work of finding more books. And that's what we were talking about. The excitement, the curiosity. I just think that is the best part of this, is that when you have that one story and sometimes, I call them the home run books. It's the books that like really get them engaged in the possibility of more reading and make them want to keep going. That's why I do it. And so I think it's that sharing as much as possible as we were building their knowledge, but then also finding those stories that make them want to say, I want more, I want to learn more, I want to read more. And those to me are the best moments.

VERA: What is one tip or piece of advice you would give to educators?

JUAN: For those educators who are on this journey of wanting to be more diverse, wanting to be more inclusive of the work that you do with literacy, just go for it. Go for it and apologize later if you need to. I think it's so important. And I think it was with you, Vera. I remember we were speaking with some educators and somebody said that when we limit the type of backgrounds that we share with our stories, then we're telling these communities of people that they're not accepted, they're not good enough. And I never want to do that in my work. And so as educators, we teach all. And so if we teach all, that means we need to show them all. And start where you can and build that, because like we said earlier, as we were speaking, it doesn't just start and it's all great in the beginning. It takes courage. It takes research. And take it step by step, but don't give up, and know that at the end of this, by being more inclusive with the stories that you share, you are developing these students that you're working with bigger than you ever imagined.

VERA: What are your top five favorite read alouds?

JUAN: This is the worst question you could ever ask anyone. So right now, I had to go to the bookshelf and pick the top five. The ones that are coming to mind right now is *After the Fall* by Dan Santat. I just think is a beautiful story of life and courage, and what it means to get back up again. And such an important topic, because now as I've grown into adulthood, sometimes I think I grew up with this idea that life was going to be easy, but really we don't talk about struggle. We don't talk about struggle enough, and that story does it beautifully. And just thinking about it, it's a good one.

Drawn Together [by Minh Lê] I think is another one that is fantastic. Just a beautiful story of communication and what it means to like find—I don't know, it's a story of... I don't know if you want a quick little book talk, but it's a beautiful story of a grandfather and a boy who couldn't find any way to relate to each other, and then find out that art is their way that they can communicate. So while there's a language barrier there, art gets them to understand each other better. And so then you were taken into this beautifully imaginative world through their illustration and how they connect. Beautiful. Beautiful.

Mr. Tiger Goes Wild [by Peter Brown] while at the very surface level can feel like a very humorous read, I love it because it's about not conforming to norms and how you don't have to do things because everyone else is doing it, and in doing so you can find yourself better. And so that's the one I love, because you can share early on and it might kind of go over their head, but when you look at it again, and really look at it deeply, it is about not conforming to the norms.

And you know, I do want to say too, as an educator, I always stick to a lot of these stories that have animals as main characters, simply because it's hard to find one where a lot of students can connect with. And sometimes when animals are the main character, it doesn't matter what gender or background they have, there's a solid like connection point. So something I was just kind of realizing as I'm running through books in my head.

My Papi Has a Motorcycle [by Isabel Quintero]. That one is not just for teaching writing, but just captures the excitement of what a parent can bring and time together. That one does it so beautifully.

I Want My Hat Back by Jon Klassen. I think that one is, again, kind of like *Mr. Tiger Goes Wild,* where you introduce them and they seem very like surface humors. But with your more developed readers, you can really dig in. That is, you can begin the discussions of the trail and being a thief and backstabbing and lies, and what that means and how that changes people's personalities and what they do. So that is one of my favorites, too, because as the readers are more developed, you can really take what feels like a simple story and really dissect it.

VERA: That's a good one. That one I love to talk to kids about perception. Like what do you think based on what we know, and how does that change throughout the story? And that anticipation. He does such a good job of the anticipation of a page turn. That's a really good book.

VERA: Do you have anything you think would be helpful or anything you want to add?

JUAN: I just think this work that you are doing and helping all of us become better rebellious readers or begin being a rebellious reader, I think is so important because keeping to the art form of literacy and what it is, it was always meant to connect and to share stories. And those stories can be ones that you identify with and stories you can identify with, but to limit that should never be the work of a teacher who teaches literacy. Because this art form was meant for us to explore all facets of the world through these authors. And so that's why we should get rebellious and not stick to the norms, and the stories that are still good, that we see being shared year after year in the education field. There's nothing wrong with them, but we should always want more, because there's so much great texts out there to find.

I wish I heard what we're talking about said to me in the beginning journey when I was making lots of mistakes, when I was making those mistakes about still labeling, still representing communities incorrectly. In the beginning of this process, the weight was so heavy that it felt like, "What am I doing? I'm so embarrassed. I don't want people to think this of me, and I don't want to hurt anyone."

But now, what I've learned about this story is it's filled with mistakes, it's filled with missteps, and you've just got to keep going because when you don't know something, mistakes are inevitable. So I think having these conversations will help so many because if you're in the beginning, you're going to make those mistakes like I did, and rather than just kind of living with the weight of it, being able to hear someone else say will help you process better to get to the next step. So I think that's why these talks are important.

VERA: I feel like the mindset of teachers feeling like you have to be the vessel of knowledge for children all the time, I thought was dispelled ages ago, but I still think we can hold onto that a little bit. And so the idea of making mistakes and being vulnerable and wrong in front of kids is kind of like, "No, no, no, no. No, you have to be right all the time." And there's no way you can.

So even if you get…we get math questions wrong, we need the book for that. We get science questions wrong. We look it up. Why wouldn't we do the same with social studies or things we're learning about different cultures or languages? Why wouldn't we go, like, "You know what? I'm not sure that's right. Let me Google that. Let me ask somebody of that culture or ask someone who speaks that language."

So if we're vulnerable in these other places, we have to be OK and show kids it's OK to do it other places as well. It has been a continual journey of, like, "Oh, I don't really know anything."

JUAN: And then in that, I'm so glad I stuck with it because there were many times where I was like, "Let me just stick to what's easy," right, because then I don't have to carry this with me. But I'm assuming I can't actually go down that route once I know better, right? It's hard. Once you know better and you want to do better, you can't ever go back.

And so having these conversations…because these journeys are always happening, always evolving. And I think that's when things like this are happening and it's new, you always want to find who else is talking about this. Who else is going through this because then you just feel connected.

VERA: And it's OK that the first year or two or three, you're just listening. It's OK that you're not always jumping in the conversation to have something to say. It's OK that you're just sitting back and taking notes. It's not…the action doesn't have to come for you right away, but that you empower yourself to create action for your students by giving them opportunities to ask questions, to be curious, to get excited, to do all the things that you'd want for yourself.

JUAN: Exactly. And I think it goes back to, and this is a whole different thing to look at, but the culture of this profession and how, where in the training of us becoming professional educators do we feel like we have to be the all-knowing being when really we are

providers of experience and knowledge. And with that comes unknowing, not knowing things and being models of that, so students know what to do when you don't know something.

And I think too, I think about now that I'm saying that how many times in my adult life have I been in a conversation and it's about a topic that I don't know. And I almost felt uncomfortable because I was afraid to say, like, "I have no idea what this is about," right? Because no one ever models what it looks like to not know something, or at least in my experience, I didn't see it that much to be comfortable in saying, "I'm not well versed in that. I have no clue," and live in it and be confident about it and not feel like it's something that makes you less [inaudible], whatever weird thoughts we have when we get comfortable.

VERA: There's a shame associated with it, and how could we know everything?

JUAN: Right.

VERA: There's no way. You're right. I do…I would love…I love…and I think it's something I should model more with my kids is I know we say there's no such thing as a stupid question, and that is true, so then how do we help kids understand that and become advocates of…or become knowledge seekers when they don't know.

I know I say to them a lot of times, like, "Well, go try it. Go figure it out. Get it wrong, and then come back to me if you still can't get it." But how do we do that with a knowledge and not just, like, "I can't get my water bottle"?

JUAN: And I think and that shows the power of printed text, because when we don't know something, now, of course, we can find the answer to it immediately through a Google search. But then as you are more developed, then you're going to find more websites to read and books and all of that as part of that reading journey of trying to be better, whatever it is that we're looking for, whatever answers we're looking for.

Notes from Classroom Conversations About Names

_____

_____

_____

_____

_____

_____

_____

_____

_____

_____

_____

_____

_____

_____

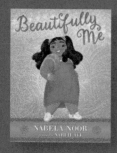

LEARNING FOR JUSTICE STANDARDS

Identity
Diversity

ELA STANDARDS

- Students will ask and answer questions about key details in a text.

- Students will acknowledge differences in the points of view of characters.

- Students will compare and contrast the adventures and experiences of characters in stories.

Features are all the physical things that make us who we are. Similar features can be shared across races and/or ethnicities. The rebellious conversations come after we identify what to do when someone is criticized or excluded because of those features. The books included in these lessons focus on features that are outside of the white/traditional/European standards. They invite conversations that ignite curious conversations.

BEAUTIFULLY ME

Written by Nabela Noor
Illustrated by Nabi H. Ali

BOOK BIOGRAPHY

Beautifully Me is a story of self-acceptance. This is also a beautiful story about body size acceptance. Zubi is so excited to start her first day of school. She puts on her favorite outfit and gets ready to start her day. But from the minute she steps into the kitchen, she is bombarded with messages of what it means to be beautiful. The problem is none of the messages match with what Zubi looks like. Can Zubi realize that she is beautiful and special for exactly who she is?

VERA'S VIEW

I'm a plus-size woman. As far back as I can remember, I've always been larger than my friends. I've never felt shamed or ostracized by my friends for my size, but I've always been aware that I didn't meet the "standard" that U.S. culture considers beautiful. How powerful this book will be for young children, to acknowledge that they are beautiful for being exactly who they are.

START SMALL

Opening pages (double spread)

What is a day that is special for you?

BE CONSISTENT

Naya is the most beautiful… (double spread)

Do you know what a diet is? Do you think children as young as Naya or Zubi should be on a diet?

At recess, some kids… (pages)

What do you think about what Kennedy says to Alix? What would you do if you heard someone say something like that? What are some ways you'd help Alix in this moment?

You get to define what is beautiful… (pages)

What is beautiful to you? How are you beautiful? How do you appreciate and celebrate the beauty in others?

KEEP CONSTANT

People come in all shapes and sizes. A "normal" body size doesn't really exist. When we see someone being treated differently or unfairly because of their body size, we should use our voice to speak up. When we see a lack of representation of body shapes and sizes, we should speak up.

LET'S MAKE A PLAN OF ACTION

- Where are the places you notice a lack of body shape inclusivity? What can you do when you notice this inclusivity?
- How do we advocate for and support people who may have been treated unkindly or unfairly because of their body shape/size?
- How do we unlearn the ways media tell us what a "good body" should look like?

Because I read this book, I now know _____ .

Because I read this book, I wonder _____ .

Because I read this book, I understand _____ .

LEARNING FOR JUSTICE STANDARDS

Identity
Diversity

ELA STANDARDS

- Students will ask and answer questions about key details in a text.

- Students will acknowledge differences in the points of view of characters.

- Students will compare and contrast the adventures and experiences of characters in stories.

BLACK IS A RAINBOW COLOR

Written by Angela Joy
Illustrated by Ekua Holmes

BOOK BIOGRAPHY

Black Is a Rainbow Color is a celebration of melanated skin and Black history and culture. The back matter is full of resources. One incredibly impactful resource is the timeline of Black ethnonyms (other words for Black throughout history).

VERA'S VIEW

I find people are often afraid to call me Black. They sometimes whisper it or look at me apologetically as if they've insulted me.

I am Black.

Sometimes children are confused when I say I'm Black. "You're not Black, you're brown," they often say. I simply tell them that Black is the term for my race but my skin color is brown.

When I was young, the only people who affirmed that my Blackness was beautiful were my family members. Media do not always portray Black women as beautiful. Children's books rarely feature Black main characters and rarely if ever highlight their Blackness. How thankful I am for books like *Black Is a Rainbow Color* that help affirm that Black is beautiful.

Black is not a dirty word.

START SMALL

Opening pages (double spread)

What is the name of your skin color?

BE CONSISTENT

Black are the braids...(double spread)

Black is a color but it is also a word used to describe a person's race/ethnicity. On these pages do you think the word *black* is used as a color or used to describe someone's race? How do you know?

Black is history...(pages)

What do you notice about the way the author uses the word *black* on these pages? Do you think the word *black* is being used to describe a color or someone's race? How do you know? How are these pages similar to or different from the "Black are the braids..." pages?

KEEP CONSTANT

Using the correct terminology when describing someone's race/ethnicity is important. It is also important to remember that no person is a representative of that race/ethnicity; you may find that different people prefer different terms to describe themselves. That's OK! If you're ever unsure, just politely ask.

LET'S MAKE A PLAN OF ACTION

- What do you think of when you think of the color word *black*?
- Do you associate the word *black* with something bad, dirty, or wrong?
- What can we do to make an effort to associate the word *black* with joy?
- How can you celebrate Blackness if you aren't Black?

Because I read this book, I now know _____.

Because I read this book, I wonder _____.

Because I read this book, I understand _____.

LEARNING FOR JUSTICE STANDARDS

Identity
Diversity
Justice
Action

ELA STANDARDS

- Students will ask and answer questions about key details in a text.

- Students will acknowledge differences in the points of view of characters.

- Students will describe how characters in a story respond to major events and challenges.

- Students will compare and contrast the adventures and experiences of characters in stories.

NOT QUITE SNOW WHITE

Written by Ashley Franklin
Illustrated by Ebony Glenn

BOOK BIOGRAPHY

Tameika wants nothing more than to sing and dance and share her talent with the world. When the time comes for school auditions for the play *Snow White*, Tameika is ready to show what she's got. But some unkind words from her peers make her question if she is good enough.

VERA'S VIEW

Not Quite Snow White debuted during a time when there was controversy over a Black woman playing the role of a mermaid in a movie. People were outraged. "Mermaids are only WHITE!" they shouted. As if a mythological creature belongs to only one race. This book is a perfect introduction to two topics: (1) no one has the right to comment on your body and (2) you can never steal away Black joy.

START SMALL

Opening pages (double spread)

What is something you love to do just for yourself?

BE CONSISTENT

After the audition… (double spread)

Why would the kids whisper those things about Tameika? What is a way you could take action in that moment? Who has the right to talk about your body?

What are other ways people of color are told they can't do something because of their skin color?

Tameika looked at her legs… (pages)

Because of the things the other kids said, Tameika has self-doubt. She is doubting that she can actually be Snow White. Was there ever a time you doubted yourself based on what someone else said? Have you ever heard someone doubt themselves before?

What would you do or say if you were on this page with Tameika?

KEEP CONSTANT

No one has the right to say anything about our bodies. Our bodies belong to ourselves. This is also why people must ask before giving us hugs, handshakes, kisses, or other forms of physical contact.

LET'S MAKE A PLAN OF ACTION

- How can you speak up if you hear someone commenting about another person's features?
- How can you speak up for yourself if someone says something negative about your body or features?
- What is a feature about yourself that you love? How can you highlight or celebrate that feature?

Because I read this book, I now know _____ .

Because I read this book, I wonder _____ .

Because I read this book, I understand _____ .

LEARNING FOR JUSTICE STANDARDS

Identity
Diversity

ELA STANDARDS

- Students will ask and answer questions about key details in a text.

- Students will acknowledge differences in the points of view of characters.

- Students will identify words and phrases in stories or poems that suggest feelings or appeal to the senses.

EYES THAT KISS IN THE CORNERS

Written by Johanna Ho
Illustrated by Dung Ho

BOOK BIOGRAPHY

A young girl embraces the beauty of her eye shape. She notices that her eye shape is similar to her mother's, her grandmother's, and her sister's. Throughout the book, she repeats that her family has eyes that "kiss in the corners and glow like warm tea." We see cultural references to food, clothing, and stories that invite us in and encourage us to learn more.

VERA'S VIEW

I am so excited to share this book. I know we focus on embracing and discussing skin color, but rarely do we see a focus on specific features. *Eyes That Kiss in the Corners* is a celebration of a feature that is often grossly misrepresented, especially in children's books. Hopefully, this book will set the standard for how to accurately illustrate eyes and how to engage the reader.

START SMALL

Opening pages (double spread)

How does the main character feel about her friend's eyes?

How do you know?

BE CONSISTENT

Three generations on the bed... (page)

The grandmother, mother, and daughter all have the same eye shape. What other features do they have in common?

Amah at tea time... (page)

Why is this an important moment for Amah and the girl?

The author repeats the line "Eyes that kiss in the corners and glow like warm tea." What do you think "glow like warm tea" means?

Why is that important for this story?

KEEP CONSTANT

Physical features are all the things that make us look the way we do. Physical features are often inherited because of genetics. Physical features like eye shape, nose shape, and hair color can be spread across different races or ethnicities.

LET'S MAKE A PLAN OF ACTION

- What can we say when we see a physical feature that is different from our own?
- How can we learn more about positive and accurate representation of physical features?
- What do we do if we see or read an inaccurate representation of physical features in the books we read?
- What do we do if we hear someone treat someone unkindly because of their physical features?

Because I read this book, I now know _____ .

Because I read this book, I wonder _____ .

Because I read this book, I understand _____ .

LEARNING FOR JUSTICE STANDARDS

Identity
Diversity

ELA STANDARDS

- Students will ask and answer questions about key details in a text.

- Students will acknowledge differences in the points of view of characters.

- Students will identify words and phrases in stories or poems that suggest feelings or appeal to the senses.

LAXMI'S MOOCH

Written by Shelly Anand
Illustrated by Nabi H. Ali

BOOK BIOGRAPHY

Laxmi's Mooch is the story of a young girl learning to embrace her features. Her classmates point out that she has hair above her lips that resembles a small "mooch," or mustache. Can Laxmi learn to embrace her mooch?

VERA'S VIEW

I'm not sure I would have thought that in my lifetime I'd see a children's book celebrating facial hair. But I am so happy it exists! This story helps normalize and celebrate facial hair.

START SMALL

Opening pages (double spread)

Laxmi is inviting us to look at her "mooch," or mustache. Do you have facial hair? What is the purpose of facial hair?

BE CONSISTENT

I do? I asked. Meow said Noah... (page)

Laxmi says, "My cheeks grew as hot as a steaming bowl of Mummy's aloo gobi," after Noah says she has a mustache. What is Laxmi feeling at this moment? What is wrong with having a mustache?

Haan, I also have a mooch... (page)

Do you know anyone with facial hair like you? Can all people have facial hair? Why or why not?

KEEP CONSTANT

Physical features are what makes us look the way we do. Physical features are often inherited because of genetics. Physical features like eye shape, nose shape, or hair color can be spread across different races or ethnicities. Physical features can also spread across genders.

LET'S MAKE A PLAN OF ACTION

- What can we say when we see a physical feature that is different from our own?
- What do we do if we hear someone treat someone unkindly because of their physical features?
- When throughout history have people faced injustice due to their physical features?

Because I read this book, I now know _____ .

Because I read this book, I wonder _____ .

Because I read this book, I understand _____ .

OUR FEATURES ARE IMPORTANT

TEACHER TALK

FEATURED EDUCATOR: Matt Halpern.

Portland, Maine. Kindergarten. Eighteen years in elementary education. LGBTQ+ educator. Pronouns: he/him.

VERA: Can you talk to me a bit about your experience with teaching "controversial" topics through read alouds?

MATT: I find them to be the best, most accessible way to allow children to experience intense emotions, ask questions, and create a sense of wonder and curiosity. The conversations that stem from these books are priceless and have opened so many important topics to my students.

VERA: What are some challenges you've faced?

MATT: Honesty, I think I've been lucky for the most part to receive very little pushback…and we've had some really tough conversations. I am always sure to let families know with a quick email about the book and conversations that followed so there are no surprises. Maybe that has helped? I did work with another teacher who received some pushback after sharing *Julian Is a Mermaid* [by Jessica Love] with her class. A parent was not happy and felt it did not "align with their family's values." Thankfully, administration was very supportive and spoke with the parent.

VERA: Why is the work of integrating "controversial" books into your daily read-aloud schedule important or meaningful to you?

MATT: I truly believe our most important job is helping our children be critical thinkers. The best way to help them learn to think for themselves is to share books with ideas and concepts that may be new to them and allow them to safely think and share their ideas about these "new to them" ideas. After reading books deemed "controversial" for years, what starts to happen is they're not so controversial anymore. The more shame and fear you give books and topics deemed "difficult," the more power they hold over you. The best way through anything difficult is by charging into the situation. Read the books. Have the conversations. Understand the power lies in guiding our students.

VERA: What have you noticed in your students/children as a result of rebellious read alouds?

MATT: The best part is the ideas and conversations started by the children, not me. Kids want to learn and talk about these ideas; we simply need to provide opportunities. Once, after reading *Who Was Rosa Parks?* [by Yona Z. McDonough], one of my students asked, "Mr. Halpern, is it OK to break a law if the law isn't a good law?" Whoa. This from a kindergartener. So I asked the class, "What do you think?" And we had the most amazing conversation about unjust and unfair laws.

VERA: What is one tip or piece of advice you would give to educators?

MATT: Take a deep breath and be brave. Seek out others in your building who feel the same. Try to gauge how your administration feels, and if they're not supportive, work on them. Read *all* the books. Lean into the discomfort. Enjoy the conversations.

VERA: What are your top five favorite read alouds?

MATT: Well, this is hard. But here are five I truly adore:

1. *Natsumi* by Susan Lendroth
2. *I Affirm Me* by Nyasha Williams
3. *Teddy's Favorite Toy* by Christian Trimmer
4. *Trouper* by Meg Kearney
5. *I Am Jazz* by Jessica Herthel

Notes from Classroom Conversations About Features

LEARNING FOR JUSTICE STANDARDS

Identity
Diversity

ELA STANDARDS

- Students will ask and answer questions about key details in a text.

- Students will acknowledge differences in the points of view of characters.

- Students will compare and contrast the adventures and experiences of characters in stories.

Most public school holidays and traditions are centered around U.S. traditions and Judeo-Christian holidays. Quite often celebrations, traditions, and holidays of other cultures or religions are left out simply because many educators don't know of or don't personally celebrate the various holidays, celebrations, and traditions observed in homes across the United States and around the world. With the lessons in this unit, I've tried to give space for young people to explore and learn about traditions that they may not have heard of before. Simultaneously, I want to validate that these traditions are important and deserve equal representation in our curriculums.

THE SHADOW IN THE MOON

A Tale of the Mid-Autumn Festival

Written by Christina Matula
Illustrated by Pearl Law

BOOK BIOGRAPHY

The Mid-Autumn Festival is also known as the Moon Festival or Mooncake festival. It is a time to give thanks and make wishes or prayers for the new year. In *The Shadow in the Moon*, we find out the history of the holiday and learn more about traditions and symbols celebrated with this holiday.

VERA'S VIEW

Sometimes, we grow up celebrating holidays or traditions because it's something our families and loved ones have done for years. What I love about this story is learning more about the Chinese tale of how the holiday came to be. Hou Yi and Chang'e's sacrifice and selflessness inspire us to reflect on the reasons we have to be thankful and hopeful for great things to come.

START SMALL

Tonight is our Mid-Autumn (double spread)

What are the holidays or traditions you celebrate that gather family and friends to your home or another special place?

BE CONSISTENT

My favorite part of dinner... (double spread)

The Moon Festival and mooncakes are connected to the story of Chang'e. Are there any foods that your family eats that have an important history?

Don't be sad my love... (page)

What Chang'e did is called sacrifice. In order to keep peace and order in the world, Chang'e drank the potion, turned immortal, and was sent to stay in the moon. To remember her and thank her for her sacrifice, Hou Yi "put out her favorite foods...to remind her that she was still in her heart." What are some ways you remember the people who were special to you?

KEEP CONSTANT

Similar to Lunar New Year, the Mid-Autumn Festival or Moon Festival is celebrated in countries other than China. The festival has different names, symbols, traditions, and tales associated with the holiday based on the specific country. When discussing traditions or holidays celebrated throughout a particular area or region, be sure to distinguish the differences/similarities between each area.

LET'S MAKE A PLAN OF ACTION

- What is a legend or tale you are inspired by?
- Who are people in history who have been selfless? How have they inspired change or action?
- How can we be respectful and thoughtful of the traditions and celebrations of people that are different from our own? Why is that important?

Because I read this book, I now know _____ .

Because I read this book, I wonder _____ .

Because I read this book, I understand _____ .

LEARNING FOR JUSTICE STANDARDS

Identity
Diversity

ELA STANDARDS

- Students will ask and answer questions about key details in a text.

- Students will acknowledge differences in the points of view of characters.

- Students will compare and contrast the adventures and experiences of characters in stories.

AMIRA'S PICTURE DAY

Written by Reem Faruqi
Illustrated by Fahmida Azim

BOOK BIOGRAPHY

The story is about Amira's excitement for the celebration of Eid, only until she realizes the day is also picture day at school! How will Amira's friends remember her if she's not in the class picture?

VERA'S VIEW

I think there are moments when students have to choose between a celebration at school versus one at home. This story is an important reminder to educators and schools to plan events, homework, and celebrations around *all* religious holidays to ensure *every* child can participate!

START SMALL

Opening pages (double spread)

Have you ever tracked the days by the cycle of the moon? Do you know any celebrations that revolve around the moon's cycle?

BE CONSISTENT

A colorful flyer on the fridge…(double spread)

What do you think Amira should do? Should she go to the Eid celebration or go to picture day at her school?

When Amira was finally ready…(pages)

Amira is wearing a special outfit called a *shalwar kameez*. Do you wear any special clothing to celebrate holidays or traditions?

KEEP CONSTANT

Eid is a celebration that happens when Ramadan ends. During Ramadan many people fast during the daytime. If you aren't someone who participates in Ramadan, it's important to remember to be thoughtful of the practices of Muslim people during this time.

LET'S MAKE A PLAN OF ACTION

- What can your school do to help ensure students don't miss picture day, or any other important day at school, when they are celebrating a tradition?
- What are some things we can do to help others feel included when they might miss out on school opportunities?
- What holidays or traditions are important to you and your family? How do you help others learn about your holidays and traditions?

Because I read this book, I now know _____ .

Because I read this book, I wonder _____ .

Because I read this book, I understand _____ .

OUR TRADITIONS ARE IMPORTANT

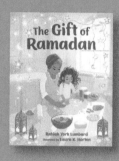

LEARNING FOR JUSTICE STANDARDS

Identity
Diversity

ELA STANDARDS

- Students will ask and answer questions about key details in a text.

- Students will acknowledge differences in the points of view of characters.

- Students will compare and contrast the adventures and experiences of characters in stories.

THE GIFT OF RAMADAN

Written by Rabiah York Lumbard
Illustrated by Laura K. Horton

BOOK BIOGRAPHY

The Gift of Ramadan is the story of young Sophia, who wants to try fasting for Ramadan for the first time. She tries so hard to stop thinking about food or eating, but it becomes too difficult and she gives in to enjoy a satisfying bite. But her grandmother shows her that there are many ways to celebrate Ramadan. Sophia explores ways to celebrate that are most meaningful to her.

VERA'S VIEW

As someone who does not celebrate Ramadan, I gained a great perspective from this story to share the traditions around Ramadan with my students. The story provides so many opportunities for students to make connections to the holidays and traditions they celebrate in their families.

START SMALL

Sophia knew that ... (double spread)

Have you ever tried to do something that took patience?

BE CONSISTENT

Sophia found Adam... (double spread)

Why do you think Adam isn't fasting? Have you ever had someone tease or taunt you when you're trying to do something? How do you get them to stop?

What is this... (pages)

Why do you think the grandmother speaks gently to Sophia when she finds her eating the cookie?

What is the name of the emotion Sophia might be feeling? It can be difficult to live up to expectations. Sometimes we can't do everything we are supposed to do. How does it feel to let someone down? Is it more important to meet expectations or allow yourself to make mistakes?

KEEP CONSTANT

When we learn about traditions or holidays that are associated with a specific religion, it's important to remember that each individual experiences that tradition or holiday in their own way. They may choose to do things exactly how they've been taught, or they may make changes that fit their own needs. Either way, we remember that every person is themselves and not a representation for an entire race, religion, or experience.

LET'S MAKE A PLAN OF ACTION

- What are some ways you can support others when they make a mistake?
- If you know someone who is fasting during Ramadan, what are some ways you can support them during the day?
- What are other ways your school or classroom can be supportive of students who are fasting during Ramadan?

Because I read this book, I now know _____.

Because I read this book, I wonder _____.

Because I read this book, I understand _____.

LEARNING FOR JUSTICE STANDARDS

Identity
Diversity

ELA STANDARDS

- Students will ask and answer questions about key details in a text.

- Students will acknowledge differences in the points of view of characters.

- Students will compare and contrast the adventures and experiences of characters in stories.

THE NIAN MONSTER

Written by Andrea Wang
Illustrated by Alina Chau

BOOK BIOGRAPHY

Xingling and her family are preparing for the arrival of Chinese New Year. As they prepare, Xingling asks her grandmother why only certain colors are used during the new year. Her grandmother gives Xingling a brief history of the Nian Monster, who would crawl out of his cave once a year and gobble up the people in the nearby town. Xingling's grandmother tells her all about the Nian Monster's weaknesses. Soon Xingling finds that information will help her save her family and her town from the Nian Monster.

VERA'S VIEW

The Nian Monster is one of my favorite stories about the Lunar New Year. This story is specifically about the Chinese New Year. The quick wit and playful nature of Xingling reminds me so much of the students in my class.

START SMALL

Opening pages (double spread)

How does your family celebrate the new year? When do you celebrate the new year? What are the colors you use to decorate for the new year?

BE CONSISTENT

Long ago…(double spread)

The story the grandmother is telling is called a *legend*. Legends are stories told (usually orally) over the course of many years. This legend of the Nian Monster helps explain why certain colors, foods, and traditions are seen during Chinese New Year. Think of some other legends you have heard. How are they similar to or different from the Nian Monster?

My stomach is too stuffed…(page)

Xingling outsmarted the monster by stuffing his stomach with a yummy meal. What other characteristics do you notice about Xingling? How do those characteristics help her throughout the story?

Nian flicked his forked tail…(page)

The characters visit different locations throughout Shanghai. Look up the different locations to learn more. How are those places similar to or different from where you live?

KEEP CONSTANT

The Lunar New Year is celebrated in different ways throughout the world. As you share stories and traditions about the various ways to celebrate the new year, be sure to differentiate between Chinese New Year and Lunar New Year. There are many other new year celebrations that occur during the spring, summer, and fall months as well. Be sure to research those specific celebrations and make efforts to integrate them into your curriculum.

LET'S MAKE A PLAN OF ACTION

- What other New Year celebrations did you learn about? How do you say Happy New Year in the languages of those celebrations?
- How can we be respectful and thoughtful of the traditions and celebrations of people that are different from our own? Why is that important?
- How and when do people in your community celebrate a new year? Is that at the same time of year as you celebrate?

Because I read this book, I now know _____ .

Because I read this book, I wonder _____ .

Because I read this book, I understand _____ .

LEARNING FOR JUSTICE STANDARDS

Identity
Diversity

ELA STANDARDS

- Students will ask and answer questions about key details in a text.

- Students will acknowledge differences in the points of view of characters.

- Students will compare and contrast the adventures and experiences of characters in stories.

OUR FAVORITE DAY OF THE YEAR

Written by A. E. Ali
Illustrated by Rahele Jomepour Bell

BOOK BIOGRAPHY

A group of students start their first day of kindergarten. Their teacher explains that they will be making new friends this year. She asks students to share their favorite day of the year with one another. Excited and a little nervous, Musa begins to share his favorite day with his new friends during lunch time. They all find that they don't have the same favorite day. Throughout the school year Musa, Moisés, Mo, and Kevin share their favorite days of the year and why those days are special to them and their families.

VERA'S VIEW

As an educator, I sometimes get caught up in trying to acknowledge or celebrate *all* holidays (even ones my students don't celebrate), and that can be a little overwhelming. I love this book because the class focuses on the diversity inside their own classroom and honors everyone's holidays and traditions throughout the year. If your classroom has more homogenous celebrations and traditions, you could use this book as an entry point to look at what other children do throughout the year rather than in just one season or month.

START SMALL

Opening pages (double spread)

How did you feel on the first day of school? Did you know anyone in your classroom? Was it easy or difficult for you to make friends? Why or why not?

BE CONSISTENT

Musa sat with Moisés, Mo and Kevin…(page)

The children are discussing their favorite holidays, but none of them are arguing that the holiday they celebrate is better. Why is that important to notice?

Eid Mubarak…(page)

Did you know of this holiday before reading this story?

Did you notice the author says, "People eat all kinds of food, since Muslims (MUSS--LIMS) come from around the world"? Why is this important to know?

Shanah Tovah…(page)

Did you know of this holiday before reading this story?

Las Posadas…(page)

Did you know of this holiday before reading this story?

Pi Day…(page)

Did you know of this holiday before reading this story?

KEEP CONSTANT

Holidays and traditions vary across cultures, religions, locations, and ethnicities. When we learn about a culture's holidays and traditions, we need to learn the difference between *appropriation* and *appreciation*. Cultural appropriation is adopting elements of one culture when a person doesn't come from that culture. It's almost as if someone borrows someone's culture without asking or understanding that culture. Cultural appreciation is learning and understanding about a culture different from yours in order to have better appreciation for people and the world.

LET'S MAKE A PLAN OF ACTION

- What can we say or do when we learn about a holiday or tradition that is different from our own?
- How can we appreciate a culture's traditions and holidays in a respectful way?
- How does our school celebrate or recognize traditions and celebrations from different cultures? How can we work to make the school more inclusive?

Because I read this book, I now know _____ .

Because I read this book, I wonder _____ .

Because I read this book, I understand _____ .

TEACHER TALK

FEATURED EDUCATOR: Shaquam Archer

Brooklyn, New York. Prekindergarten. Over eighteen years teaching early childhood education. Black educator. Pronouns: she/her.

VERA: Can you talk to me a bit about your experience with teaching "controversial" topics through read alouds?

SHAQUAM: I've always enjoyed highlighting controversial topics specifically related to social justice. Controversy lives there. To start each school year I read *The Story of Ruby Bridges* [by Robert Coles]. This is the time of year to develop our class family by thinking about who we are as beings, what groups we belong to, what it means to belong to a group, and what our behaviors/habits/attitudes should sound and look like in order for our class family to become what we need it to be. I choose this story each year because it is relatable to young children who see themselves in this little girl who just wanted equal rights, to belong to her peer group, and attend school to learn new things. We talk about Ruby's strength and hopes, how she saw herself as capable and deserving. We discuss how she was treated as a human and then we use our thoughts and ideas to write individual letters to Ruby imagining her being a student entering our class today. Each year the responses are varied, but last year our students also felt strongly about writing a collaborative letter to "the mean/angry people." We wrote our letters. In the past I've taken dictation and printed the letters alongside drawings, but this year we ink transferred the letters onto broken sheet rock slabs so that I could hang them as a permanent fixture in my classroom. After writing our letters, we establish classroom rules, promises, expectations, and we hold ourselves and each other accountable with a picture of Ruby attached to our final list so we do not forget our inspiration. Stories like Ruby's have become a staple in my curriculum year after year. I can't wait until an assigned time to teach the children that historical controversy is what shaped our lives today. It is essential.

VERA: What are some challenges you've faced?

SHAQUAM: Over the last two years I worked in Williamsburg, Brooklyn, at a private institution where I am one of one black teachers in a leadership role. There are even fewer students of color, and the few identify as mixed race. When I introduced the Ruby Bridges project, it was with intention that it was never highlighted in the central blogs or newsletters as other less meaningful projects were; instead, it was sheltered and surfaced toward the end of the year as part of an art exhibit. It stood alone, in the back, while other projects beamed with bright colors and signs saying "LOOK AT ME!" After the exhibit was over, the project disappeared, and I had to ask about its whereabouts. I was told that it was decided by administrators and the art teacher (all white) that it would be permanently displayed in an area of the school as a symbol of antiracism. Excuse me…my project that I actually decided would hang in my own classroom for as long as I worked here to remind me of why my work is important. So the next day it was returned to me without a follow-up conversation.

It was offensive and something that I've never experienced. I guess the short answer to this question is that people don't want to do the actual work but want to somehow take credit for the exposure. Deep sigh…I am again bothered in this moment.

I've also had caregivers ask me to pull back because they did not know how to confront topics at home.

VERA: Why is the work of integrating "controversial" books into your daily read-aloud schedule important or meaningful to you?

SHAQUAM: I have always been interested in how culture, as both constraining and enabling, affects early childhood education. The triad of poverty, racism, and a subpar education system has always been at the forefront of my teaching philosophy and practices. Being an educator of color who has primarily serviced communities with very few people of color happened by accident, but as the years went by I decided that it's where I should be positioned. I think it is important for POC [people of color] to show up as leaders in communities that are largely made up of non-POC. I also continue every year to develop practices and curricula that will teach young children concrete life skills, specifically critical thinking and problem-solving skills so that they will be equipped to make healthy decisions throughout adolescence and adulthood, so they need healthy controversy. The exposure of controversy creates the potential for our students to develop into thoughtful and intentional leaders taking ownership over their own learning and building social skills. They learn to belong to a group where it is required for them to be present, respect differences, and see everyone's input as meaningful and valuable, even if we agree to disagree with a conclusion that spotlights an important piece of understanding our work. The quality of these early experiences shapes social, cognitive, and emotional aptitude. I also believe as an educator it is very important to help students to see the world as current and real.

VERA: What have you noticed in your students/children as a result of rebellious read alouds?

SHAQUAM: I am very animated and excitable, and so when I set the tone in spaces where I teach, students always adapt and exude the same energy and excitement for not only making their voices heard but feeling confident that their voices are valued in their space. They learn to be active listeners with a mutual respect for the idea of compromise, integrity, individual truth, and a growth mindset.

Since my students are fairly young, we often start with the "What would you rather?" activity. Two choices are presented to the entire group, each student makes a personal choice based on interests, and then we split into two groups to discuss our viewpoints. Here's an example: What would you rather have as a pet: a dragon or dinosaur? Such great choices! Students make their choices, we split into two groups, and each group discusses why they made their choice. Both groups then face each other and talk about their choices to each other; sometimes they find commonalities and sometimes not, and we make sure to highlight the idea that it's OK to make different choices.

This activity helps us practice for more controversial topics/choices. I don't only use children's literature. I also try to include as many current event topics that directly relate to children their age. I would clip photos out of the local newspaper and put them in a general place where students can see and ask questions, and I never give political context. During Trump's reign of terror there were so many questions about the young children separated at the border. "Where are their parents?" "Why is she alone?" "Who put them there?" "Are their mommies coming back?" "This picture makes me feel sad." "If I was there..."

There are so many wonderful ways to make controversy an important part of our curriculum.

VERA: What is one tip or piece of advice you would give to educators?

SHAQUAM: It is important for educators to take risks for the sake of humanity.

VERA: What are your top 5 favorite read alouds?

SHAQUAM:

1. *The Story of Ruby Bridges* by Robert Coles
2. *And Tango Makes Three* by Henry Cole
3. *Drum Dream Girl* by Margarita Engle
4. *A Kids Book About Racism* by Jelani Memory
5. *Strictly No Elephants* by Lisa Mantchev

OUR ACTIONS ARE IMPORTANT

LEARNING FOR JUSTICE STANDARDS

Identity
Diversity
Justice
Action

ELA STANDARDS

- Students will ask and answer questions about key details in a text.

- Students will acknowledge differences in the points of view of characters.

- Students will describe how characters in a story respond to major events and challenges.

The action books tend to make some of my favorite lessons. They take us from the abstract to the concrete and encourage our students to be the change they want to see. The books in this unit invite students to look for those opportunities to be independently inclusive. My hope is that as children grow through their education career and into adulthood, they continue to look for moments to be allies.

ALEJANDRIA FIGHTS BACK!

¡La Lucha de Alejandria!
By/por Leticia Hernández-Linares and the Rise-Home Stories Project
Illustrated by/ilustrado por Robert Liu-Trujillo
Translated by/traducido por Carla España

BOOK BIOGRAPHY

Alejandria loves her neighborhood. One day she notices there are more and more "For Sale" signs posted along her street. She sees moving boxes in her friend's apartment. She notices her mom upset about a notice left on their door. Alejandria learns that her building's landlord is increasing the rent to force families out so the building can be sold at a higher price. Alejandria knows that something must be done. Can she find a way to use her voice to make a difference?

VERA'S VIEW

Home stability is a concern that affects our students whether we think they are aware of it or not. Living in New York during the height of the pandemic, I watched as many of my students and their families relocated to more affordable locations as adults lost their jobs and landlords continued to demand rent. It wasn't until an eviction freeze was put into place that families could begin to feel a bit of relief. What I love about *Alejandria Fights Back* is that we see her recognize an issue, learn more about her rights, elicit help, feel scared and intimidated, and still stand up for what's right.

START SMALL

Welcome to Parkwood... (double spread)

Where do you live? Who are the people who live in your neighborhood?

BE CONSISTENT

The next day, I heard... (page 10)

A landlord is someone who owns a building where people work or live. A landlord is responsible for keeping the building safe and clean. A landlord charges rent for people to work or live in the building they own. Some landlords can be unfair or even cruel. Julian's family can no longer afford the rent in their building. The landlord increasing the rent means Julian's family might have to find a new place to live. Julian might have to move schools.

What are the other ways a student or their family could be affected by a landlord increasing the rent?

Tita always says... (page 21)

Before Alejandria starts taking direct action against the rising rent, she and her Tita go to the library to learn more about their rights. Why is it important to gather more information before making a decision? How is it helpful to have more information when speaking up for what is right? Where are the places you can go to learn more information?

When we got to city hall... (page 32)

Have you ever felt nervous or scared before speaking up for what's right?

KEEP CONSTANT

We don't always know all the rights we have. When those rights are violated or put into question, it's important to learn as much as possible in order to stand up for ourselves and others. It is important to continue to learn about and speak up for our rights.

LET'S MAKE A PLAN OF ACTION

- What are some ways you can support people in your community who may be facing eviction?
- What can we do if we notice someone is scared or feels intimated to use their voice to speak up for what's right? How can we support them?
- What are the ways your neighborhood has changed over time? How have those changes positively or negatively affected you or your family? How have those changes positively or negatively affected people who are different from you? What can you do to help?

Because I read this book, I now know _____.

Because I read this book, I wonder _____.

Because I read this book, I understand _____.

OUR ACTIONS ARE IMPORTANT

LEARNING FOR JUSTICE STANDARDS

Identity
Diversity
Justice
Action

ELA STANDARDS

- Students will ask and answer questions about key details in a text.

- Students will acknowledge differences in the points of view of characters.

- Students will describe how characters in a story respond to major events and challenges.

MALALA'S MAGIC PENCIL

Written by Malala Yousafzai
Illustrated by Kerascoët

BOOK BIOGRAPHY

Many adults are familiar with the story of Nobel Prize winner Malala Yousafzai. But very few young children know the amazing story of young Malala, who grew up in Pakistan. She was lucky enough to attend school and loved to learn. Her city was overtaken by members of the Taliban. The Taliban did not allow women or girls to attend school. Malala did not think that was fair or equitable. She used her voice to speak up for what she believed was right.

VERA'S VIEW

Malala's commitment to speaking up for what's right despite the costs is admirable. I wish I'd had her courage and strength when I was her age. Her voice is an inspiration to young people everywhere. Keep speaking up, keep using your voice, continue to do what you know is right, no matter what.

START SMALL

When I was younger… (double spread)

What would you do if you had a magic pencil?

BE CONSISTENT

One day, I was… (page)

What do you notice about this page? What do you think Malala is thinking? What do you think the children are thinking?

Once I started… (double spread)

Why is it important for Malala to speak up? Why is it important that she is using her voice right now, during the Taliban occupation?

I am Malala…. (double spread)

Can you think of other examples of people using their voice to make change?

KEEP CONSTANT

Sometimes, when people don't want others to use their voices to speak up for what's right, they might use violence to keep that person quiet. Violence is always wrong. Speaking up for what's right is always the right thing to do.

LET'S MAKE A PLAN OF ACTION

- What are the different ways we can use our voices?
- How do we use our voices when we feel scared or unsure?
- When have people in history used their voice to help me (suffragettes, civil rights movement, etc.)?

Because I read this book, I now know _____.

Because I read this book, I wonder _____.

Because I read this book, I understand _____.

OUR ACTIONS ARE IMPORTANT

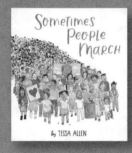

LEARNING FOR JUSTICE STANDARDS

Identity
Diversity
Justice
Action

ELA STANDARDS

- Students will ask and answer questions about key details in a text.

- Students will acknowledge differences in the points of view of characters.

- Students will describe how characters in a story respond to major events and challenges.

- Students will compare and contrast the adventures and experiences of characters in stories.

> ### SOMETIMES PEOPLE MARCH

Written and illustrated by Tessa Allen

BOOK BIOGRAPHY

Sometimes People March is a story about action. In the book, we see the different ways throughout history that people have marched for change. In a very simple but poignant way, *Sometimes People March* teaches young children that they too can make a difference.

VERA'S VIEW

In my fifteen-plus years of teaching, I've never heard more children talk about the marches or protests they've participated in than I have recently. It's exciting to hear families incorporating their children into their activism. I feel it's important to show students that activism can also happen in the classroom. There are systems and behaviors that need to be changed everywhere, and children have a voice that can inspire and enact change.

START SMALL

Marching is something… (page 8)

Have you ever marched in a protest?

BE CONSISTENT

Marching is something… (page 8)

What do you think the word *injustice* means?

The parade or march in this picture happened in 1917 and was called the New York City NAACP Silent Protest Parade. What do we know about America's treatment of Black people that can help us understand what this march may have been about?

Sometimes people carry signs… (pages)

Take a look at the signs on this page. What are some signs that stand out to you?

Are there any signs that connect with you personally? Are there any signs you have questions about?

How do signs play a part in marching?

KEEP CONSTANT

Marching or attending protests is just one way to take action for something you believe in. Marching is an important way to take action because when you work with your community for change, everyone benefits.

LET'S MAKE A PLAN OF ACTION

- How have you taken action against something you thought was wrong or unjust?
- How can you help people in your family or community speak up against injustice?
- Taking action can be big, like organizing a march, or small, like writing a letter to your community leaders. Either way, action is important. Try to be consistent with the different ways you can take action.

Because I read this book, I now know _____.

Because I read this book, I wonder _____.

Because I read this book, I understand _____.

WE ARE WATER PROTECTORS

Written by Carole Lindstrom
Illustrated by Michaela Goade

BOOK BIOGRAPHY

A water protector is someone who is an activist who works to protect and defend the world's natural water and water systems. There are many Indigenous peoples who continue to fight for the safety and protection of water. In *We Are Water Protectors*, through the eyes of a young Indigenous girl, we learn the history of the importance of water protectors and how we all must work together to keep our water clean.

VERA'S VIEW

We Are Water Protectors is such a beautifully illustrated story about how we all owe the Earth action. We all have a role in protecting and keeping our water safe from pollution and companies that demand access to sacred land.

We often hear about the importance of saving the Earth through the voice and perspective of white people. *We Are Water Protectors* is a beautiful reminder of the importance and strength of Indigenous voices.

START SMALL

Opening pages (double spread)

The author says that water is "the first medicine." What do you think that means? In what ways is water important in your life?

BE CONSISTENT

We stand with our songs... (page)

Who do you see on this page? Who is the "we" the girl is speaking about? Why is it important to notice that they are saying, "We are still here"?

Now the black snake is here... (page)

What do you think the black snake is? Why is it important for people to protect the land and water from the black snake? What could happen if people don't work together to protect the water?

KEEP CONSTANT

Taking action is not always easy. Sometimes taking action means standing alone. Sometimes taking action means gathering friends and family to help. But taking action is always important, especially when you want to change things for the greater good.

LET'S MAKE A PLAN OF ACTION

- In what ways do we have access to clean water that makes life easier for us?
- In what ways do others not have access to clean water that makes life difficult for them?
- How can we take action to help ensure everyone has access to clean water?
- What can we do to let people know the importance of taking action to protect our Earth's water?

Because I read this book, I now know _____ .

Because I read this book, I wonder _____ .

Because I read this book, I understand _____ .

OUR ACTIONS ARE IMPORTANT

LEARNING FOR JUSTICE STANDARDS

Identity
Diversity
Action

ELA STANDARDS

- Students will ask and answer questions about key details in a text.

- Students will acknowledge differences in the points of view of characters.

- Students will compare and contrast the adventures and experiences of characters in stories.

- Students will describe how characters in a story respond to major events and challenges.

EVELYN DEL REY IS MOVING AWAY

Written by Meg Medina
Illustrated by Sonia Sánchez

BOOK BIOGRAPHY

Evelyn is Daniela's *mejor amiga*, or best friend. But today everything will change because today Evelyn is moving away. They spend her last day doing all of their favorite things and making plans for how they will stay in touch even after Evelyn moves away. It is a beautiful story about the power of friendship through distance and time.

VERA'S VIEW

Children will immediately connect to this story of friendship. Children who have had to move will connect to the heartbreak of leaving friends and the nervousness of making new ones. When I left Austin, Texas, to move to Massachusetts, I moved out of state for the first time in my life. Leaving Austin meant I would be leaving some of my closest friends. I thoroughly related to the heartbreak Daniela and Evelyn felt leaving each other, unsure but hopeful that their friendship would survive both distance and time. My *mejor amiga* and I are still very close, with matching heart tattoos to commemorate our friendship.

START SMALL

Opening pages (double spread)

What is the feeling you feel when you think of your very best friend? Why is that person your best friend?

BE CONSISTENT

But the walls in Evelyn's room… (page)

Where do you think the characters live? Is it a city, a suburb, is it out in the country? Why is the location important to this story? Does the location change what we think about the characters?

Before we leave… (page)

As Evelyn leaves, the girls put stickers on their faces to "seal our promise." What promise do you think the girls made to each other? What does it mean to promise something to a friend?

KEEP CONSTANT

Friendships change. Some friends are friends for a short time; some friends are friends for a very long time. Friendships are important because friends support who we are and help us become better people.

LET'S MAKE A PLAN OF ACTION

- What are some ways you are a supportive friend?
- How do you help your friends make good choices?
- What would you do if you saw your friend being made fun of or being excluded because of who they are?

Because I read this book, I now know _____ .

Because I read this book, I wonder _____ .

Because I read this book, I understand _____ .

TEACHER TALK

FEATURED EDUCATOR: Ha Dinh.

First grade. Fifteen years in education. BIPOC educator—the global majority. Pronouns: she/her.

VERA: Can you talk to me a bit about your experience with teaching "controversial" topics through read alouds?

HA: I never thought of teaching my students to love and respect each other as "controversial" topics. To me, it has always been about building a strong community of diverse learners who are supportive, understanding, and empathetic to each other and those around them. Luckily, there are so many picture books that have helped my students learn just that, especially with more recently published books that are more inclusive of representations.

VERA: What are some challenges you've faced?

HA: From my experience, my students and their families love and appreciate books that represent them. I do my best to include representations and experiences of all my students as best as I can, and they very much appreciate being celebrated, represented, and seen.

VERA: Why is the work of integrating "controversial" books into your daily read-aloud schedule important or meaningful to you?

HA: As an Asian American, I grew up desiring to read books that represented my experiences, people, and culture. Not having access to such literature made me feel insignificant, unworthy, and unseen.

Therefore, it is extremely important for me to make sure my students know that I see and acknowledge who they are as individuals and that they are seen through our read alouds.

VERA: What have you noticed in your students/ children as a result of rebellious read alouds?

HA: My students love and crave books that help them to understand different perspectives and walks of life. It helps them to become more caring and empathic individuals and citizens of the world.

VERA: What is one tip or piece of advice you would give to educators?

HA: Building a strong community of learners begins on day one. When students feel loved, seen, and respected, especially in the books that are read to them, they will feel more successful as learners and individuals.

VERA: What are your top five favorite read alouds?

HA:

1. *All Are Welcome* by Alexandra Penfold
2. *Eyes That Kiss in the Corners* by Joanna Ho
3. *You Are Enough* by Grace Byers
4. *Where Are You From*? by Yamile Saied Méndez
5. *The Name Jar* by Yangsook Choi

Notes from Classroom Conversations About Actions

OUR FAMILIES ARE IMPORTANT

LEARNING FOR JUSTICE STANDARDS

Identity
Diversity

ELA STANDARDS

- Students will ask and answer questions about key details in a text.

- Students will acknowledge differences in the points of view of characters.

- Students will compare and contrast the adventures and experiences of characters in stories.

I'm sure you're thinking, "Of course they are, Vera." But are all families represented in your conversations around families? How do we give space to invite our students to understand that families look all kinds of ways? These books help your students discuss the ways our families disappoint us, too. Our families can disappoint us, bring us joy, teach us how to understand the world, and encourage us to be our true selves.

WHERE THREE OCEANS MEET

Written by Rajani LaRocca
Illustrated by Archana Sreenivasan

BOOK BIOGRAPHY

Where Three Oceans Meet is the story of three generations of a family traveling to India. Along the way the three think of all the things they want to do together. *Where Three Oceans Meet* is a story of family and connectedness.

VERA'S VIEW

I *loved* this book the first time I read it. I love intergenerational stories. But as I prepped for this lesson, I read it again and the deeper meaning of the title went off like a lightbulb. The title has both a metaphorical and literal meaning. These three generations of people, although they are each very different, have found their commonality, the place where they fit together, their love for one another.

START SMALL
Opening pages (double spread)
Where have you traveled before? Have you ever traveled with your family?

BE CONSISTENT

Pati and Mommy speak Tamil… (double spread)

What language do you speak at home? Is it a different language than what you speak at school? What different languages do members of your family know?

Mommy is tallest… (double spread)

What do you notice about the clothes the different family members wear? How do the clothes change from each generation to the next? How is that similar to the languages each person speaks?

She shows me how to… (double spread)

How do you style or wear your hair? Is it similar to how a family member does their hair? Has a family member ever taught you how to do something before?

KEEP CONSTANT

Each generation passes down information, traditions, language, and more. Sometimes, the distance between each generation can grow greater and greater as expectations, social norms, and history change. Families find unique ways to stay in touch with their culture and traditions despite these changes.

LET'S MAKE A PLAN OF ACTION

- How do we respect and appreciate a person's culture or history even though it may be very different from our own?
- How can we honor the traditions and culture of a place we are traveling to or visiting?
- Research the different ways goods were moved throughout the world (historical trade routes like the Silk Road). How has having access to materials and goods from other places influenced and changed our current way of life? How can we acknowledge and recognize the importance of these places?

Because I read this book, I now know _____ .

Because I read this book, I wonder _____ .

Because I read this book, I understand _____ .

LEARNING FOR JUSTICE STANDARDS

....

Identity
Diversity

ELA STANDARDS

....

- Students will
  ask and answer
  questions about
  key details
  in a text.

- Students will
  acknowledge
  differences in the
  points of view
  of characters.

- Students will
  compare and
  contrast the
  adventures and
  experiences
  of characters
  in stories.

HAIR TWINS

Written by Raakhee Mirchandani
Illustrated by Holly Hatam

BOOK BIOGRAPHY

Hair Twins is the story of a special bond between a father and daughter, whose family is Sikh. The two of them share very special moments around their hair.

VERA'S VIEW

There are many reasons to love this story. First, this is one of very few stories featuring a Sikh family, and it is a lovely introduction to a conversation around Sikhism. Second, I love a story that focuses on simple, everyday topics between a father and daughter. This would be a beautiful book to partner with *Hair Love*.

START SMALL

Opening pages (double spread)

How do you take care of your hair? What's your favorite way to style or wear your hair?

BE CONSISTENT

When Papa combs his hair... (double spread)

What do you notice about the father's hair? His hair is very long. Some people who are Sikhs don't cut their hair.

Anyone can have long hair. Anyone can have short hair.

Before we leave... (double spread)

What do you notice about the father's routine for putting his hair in his turban? Do you know of any other types of head coverings? Are there any types of head coverings you or your family wear?

Keep Constant

Hair style is one form of expression. People can wear their hair any way that makes them feel happy and comfortable. For years, Black and brown people have been told the way they style their hair isn't "correct" or is "unprofessional." But really there is no wrong way to wear or style hair.

Let's Make a Plan of Action

- What can you do to support a classmate who might have a new haircut or hair style?
- In what ways can we stand up for friends who are treated unkindly for their hair styles?
- How can you learn more about the way different cultures style their hair or use head coverings?

Because I read this book, I now know _____ .

Because I read this book, I wonder _____ .

Because I read this book, I understand _____ .

LEARNING FOR JUSTICE STANDARDS

Identity
Diversity

ELA STANDARDS

- Students will ask and answer questions about key details in a text.

- Students will acknowledge differences in the points of view of characters.

- Students will describe how characters in a story respond to major events and challenges.

- Students will compare and contrast the adventures and experiences of characters in stories.

GRANDPA GRUMPS

Written by Katrina Moore
Illustrated by Xindi Yan

BOOK BIOGRAPHY

Daisy cannot wait for Grandpa to visit from China. She has some exciting adventures for them to go on together. However, Grandpa doesn't seem to be interested in the things Daisy has planned for them. How can Daisy find a way to have fun with Grandpa before he leaves?

VERA'S VIEW

I love multigenerational stories. I grew up on the same street as my grandparents and spent many summers going on adventures with them. *Grandpa Grumps* is one of those stories that reminds us that there is always a way to connect with one another.

START SMALL

Opening pages (double spread)

Have you ever had someone special come to visit? How did that make you feel?

BE CONSISTENT

On Monday… (double spread)

Daisy keeps trying to engage Yeh-Yeh in different activities. But he doesn't seem interested. How do you start a conversation with someone who seems different from you?

On Saturday… (pages)

What was Yeh-Yeh's gift to Daisy? How did their relationship change once he was able to communicate with her?

KEEP CONSTANT

Not only can families look different on the outside, they can be different within. Members of families can speak different languages, have different skin colors, practice different religions, and live in different places from each other. While it can be challenging or take time, learning how to communicate with each other is an important part of building strong relationships with family members.

LET'S MAKE A PLAN OF ACTION

- How do you interact with your family when you don't agree with them?
- What can you say to your family when they do or say something that you disagree with?
- How can you help your family learn new ideas or try new activities?

Because I read this book, I now know _____.

Because I read this book, I wonder _____.

Because I read this book, I understand _____.

OUR FAMILIES ARE IMPORTANT

LEARNING FOR JUSTICE STANDARDS

Identity
Diversity
Justice

ELA STANDARDS

- Students will ask and answer questions about key details in a text.

- Students will acknowledge differences in the points of view of characters.

- Students will describe how characters in a story respond to major events and challenges.

A DIFFERENT POND

Written by Bao Phi
Illustrated by Thi But

BOOK BIOGRAPHY

A Different Pond is a story of a young boy's very early morning fishing trips in Minneapolis with his father. The story is a day in the life of a refugee family doing everything possible to ensure their happiness and success.

VERA'S VIEW

A Different Pond, which was written and illustrated by Vietnamese refugees, remains one of the most engaging read alouds I've seen in a long time. There are so many discussion opportunities around culture, food, youth, and history. The story reads similar to a comic book or graphic novel, with inserts and panels splattered throughout the book.

START SMALL

Opening pages (double spread)

What are some ways you help your family? How does it make you feel to help your family?

BE CONSISTENT

A kid at my school... (page 4)

What would you do if you heard someone say the way your family spoke sounded different or weird? What could you do if you heard someone say that about your friend's family?

I used to fish by a pond... (pages)

What do you think happened to the father's brother? In what ways are these fishing trips important or meaningful to the dad and the son?

I'm sad that she and dad must leave... (pages)

How does this family take care of each other? What are the different jobs the family members have?

KEEP CONSTANT

A refugee is someone who leaves their home country to avoid violence, crime, or natural disasters. Usually it is unsafe for a refugee to ever return to their home country. What a difficult decision it must be for a family or person to leave their country and risk everything for a new life somewhere unknown. In their new country, some refugees may work multiple jobs to take care of their needs (housing, food, etc.).

LET'S MAKE A PLAN OF ACTION

- What do you do if someone makes fun of the way another person speaks?
- What are some ways you can support refugees in your own community?
- Learn about the ways refugees make up the workforce in the United States. Look into programs like the DREAM Act. How can you take action to support the refugee community in your area?

Because I read this book, I now know _____ .

Because I read this book, I wonder _____ .

Because I read this book, I understand _____ .

LEARNING FOR JUSTICE STANDARDS

Identity
Diversity

ELA STANDARDS

- Students will ask and answer questions about key details in a text.

- Students will acknowledge differences in the points of view of characters.

- Students will compare and contrast the adventures and experiences of characters in stories.

SATURDAY

Written and illustrated by Oge Mora

BOOK BIOGRAPHY

Ava's mom is very busy with work during the week. But Saturdays—Saturdays were a special day for just the two of them. Ava couldn't wait to spend the day with her mom. Her mom had a full day of exciting activities planned. As soon as their day together started, everything started to go wrong. Suddenly, their favorite day turned into their worst day.

VERA'S VIEW

I was raised by a single mother. While teaching high school English, she took night courses to earn her master's degree. She worked hard to provide for me and be an amazing role model. I love this story because we don't feel bad for Ava because she comes from a single parent home. We feel bad (and connect) because we all know what it's like for plans to go terribly wrong. And we know the strength it takes to try again the next time.

START SMALL

Opening pages (double spread)

The author says, "Saturday was the day they cherished." What does the word *cherish* mean? What is something you cherish?

BE CONSISTENT

Today will be ruined if we miss that bus… (page)

Where do you think the characters live? Is it a city, a suburb, is it out in the country? Why is it important to notice that they take the bus to get to where they need to go? Why might it be stressful to rely on public transportation to commute to places?

As Ava watched… (page)

Ava's mom is frustrated that nothing is going right on their Saturday together. Why is this a frustrating moment for Ava's mom?

Ava was quiet for a moment… (page)

Throughout the story, when things go wrong, Ava's mom stops, closes her eyes, and lets out a deep breath. Why is modeling this calming strategy an important lesson for Ava? What do you do when you get frustrated?

KEEP CONSTANT

All families are different. Families should love and support one another. It is important to understand different family structures as it helps us understand one another.

LET'S MAKE A PLAN OF ACTION

- What are some different family structures you've read about? How are those structures different or similar to your own?
- How can we change our language to be sure we are inclusive when talking about families (*mommy and daddy* vs. *grown-ups*)?
- Is your school inclusive of all families? What are the words and actions your school uses to help you know that all different kinds of families are welcome?

Because I read this book, I now know _____ .

Because I read this book, I wonder _____ .

Because I read this book, I understand _____ .

TEACHER TALK

FEATURED PARENT: Marisa Dittmer

San Francisco Bay Area, California. Stay-at-home parent. White/cisgender/hetero woman. Parent of three young children (ages 2, 6, and 8). Pronouns: she/her.

VERA: Can you talk to me a bit about your experience with discussing "controversial" topics through read alouds?

MARISA: I love read alouds for that exact reason. It makes it so easy to discuss and answer questions. We have read aloud together since the kids were little, and even though my older one devours books herself, we still all read together nightly before bed. My eight-year-old is very curious about everything, so she is always asking questions when we read. We've discussed many aspects of racism, feminism, LGBTQ families, refugees, and basic aspects of colonization and Indigenous people.

VERA: What are some challenges you've faced?

MARISA: My husband at times (but not too often) feels like maybe I'm addressing topics or issues too early. He had a hard time this past year when I got rid of our Dr. Seuss books and when we discussed the reality of Thanksgiving. He knows he can share his opinion, but I will do what I want. My mom carries a lot of biases and racist ideas. Much of that has caused our barely-holding-together relationship to fully fray. (For example, she thinks if my boy wears nail polish or wears a princess costume "he'll be gay.")

VERA: Why is the work of integrating "controversial" books into your child's life important or meaningful to you?

MARISA: My one hope for my children is that they grow to be empathetic, inclusive, understanding humans who stand up for those who are marginalized. In these younger years, home is the place where I have the most control over what they will be exposed to. The younger they learn about these "controversial" topics, the easier it will be for them to navigate school, friends, life when they encounter them. I know my children hold a lot of privilege in many areas, and I want a family culture where we understand that and learn how to belong to one another in our communities and world.

VERA: What have you noticed from your children as a result of rebellious read alouds?

MARISA: They bring things up all the time! It makes my heart burst. Whether it's seeing a photo of John Lewis and knowing who he was or asking a question about someone's culture or talking about melanin in different types of skin. I am always shocked at how much they retain and remember. Even their language has changed (for example, using the term *enslaved person* instead of *slave*). They now look for and notice what we have discussed, and it has allowed for constant family dialogue.

VERA: What is one tip or piece of advice you would give to parents/caregivers?

MARISA: Don't be afraid to discuss serious and timely topics with your little ones. They are so aware and have such open hearts and minds. Don't be overwhelmed or think you need every detail and a full-on lesson plan—just start conversations, answer questions (look up answers together if you don't know them!), and trust them and yourself.

VERA: What are your top five favorite read alouds?

MARISA: I realize some of these are probably not as "rebellious," but they were the ones that came to mind and that we own and read often.

- *Four Feet, Two Sandals* by Karen Lynn Williams and Khadra Mohammed

- *Let's Talk About Race* by Julius Lester

- *Last Stop on Market Street* by Matt de la Peña

- *When You Trap a Tiger* by Tae Keller (young adult chapter book, *so* good!)

OUR IDENTITIES ARE IMPORTANT

LEARNING FOR JUSTICE STANDARDS

Identity
Diversity

ELA STANDARDS

- Students will ask and answer questions about key details in a text.

- Students will acknowledge differences in the points of view of characters.

- Students will describe how characters in a story respond to major events and challenges.

- *An Angel Like Me* by Mary Hoffman (a Christmas book we read every year)

One of my most favorite things about being an educator is watching young people understand and develop a sense of their self-identity. The books in this unit invite young people to ask questions about what they notice about the perceived identity of the characters in the story. How do these characters navigate establishing their personal identity and inviting their family or friends to embrace and accept their true selves? The lessons here help give meaning to the words we use around identity.

ARELI IS A DREAMER: A TRUE STORY

Written by Areli Morales
Illustrated by Luisa Uribe

BOOK BIOGRAPHY

Areli was born in Mexico. She spent her early years with her grandmother and brother. While Areli and her brother were in Mexico, their mother and father were in New York City working to ensure their kids would have everything they needed to start a new life. Can Areli learn to love New York City in the same way she loved her home in Mexico?

VERA'S VIEW

When I think about immigration, I think about the wealth of knowledge, stories, food, culture, language, and more that people bring from their home countries. I think of all the different ways our ancestors came to or already inhabited the United States. Despite the way our ancestors arrived here, whether by force (enslavement) or immigration, or if they were the people who originally inhabited this land, we bring out strengths together to make the United States a unique place.

START SMALL

Opening pages (double spread)

What are some games you like to play? Who do you like to play with?

BE CONSISTENT

When Areli hung up the phone… (double spread)

Where were you born? Do you still live in the place where you were born? How does where you were born or where you live become part of your identity?

The next Saturday night's dinner… (pages)

Have you had to say goodbye to someone you loved before?

Pages picturing Areli traveling from Mexico to New York City (no text—double spread)

What do you notice about these two pages? How are they different? How are they similar? Are either of these places similar to where you live?

Areli's an illegal… (page)

What would you do if you heard someone say the things the students said to Areli? Is it possible for a person to be illegal?

KEEP CONSTANT

Immigration is the act of moving from one country to another country, with the intention or hope to live in that new country. Immigration happens all over the world. Some people immigrate to start a new life in a new place. Some people are refugee immigrants. A refugee immigrant is someone who was forced to leave their country due to war, violence, persecution, or natural disaster. Different countries have different rules about how immigrants become citizens of the new country they live in. Immigrants bring their identity (culture, food, language, religion, and more) to the new country they inhabit. They add their voice and perspective to their new country.

LET'S MAKE A PLAN OF ACTION

- How can you help immigrants feel welcome in the place where you live?
- What are some different ways a person immigrates to a new country? How can we help ensure immigrants arrive to our country safely?
- What are the laws in our country that help immigrants? What are the laws in our country that hurt immigrants? How can we work to change the laws that are hurtful?

If you would like information on what Deferred Action for Childhood Arrivals (DACA) is, visit https://www.boundless.com/immigration-resources/what-is-daca/.

Because I read this book, I now know _____ .

Because I read this book, I wonder _____ .

Because I read this book, I understand _____ .

LEARNING FOR JUSTICE STANDARDS

Identity
Diversity
Justice
Action

ELA STANDARDS

- Students will ask and answer questions about key details in a text.

- Students will acknowledge differences in the points of view of characters.

- Students will describe how characters in a story respond to major events and challenges.

ALL BECAUSE YOU MATTER

Written by Tami Charles
Illustrated by Bryan Collier

BOOK BIOGRAPHY

Black, Indigenous, and children of color walk through a world that consistently tells them they are not enough, or sometimes even that they don't matter. In an ode to her own child, Tami Charles shows a young Black boy just how much he matters. Even when he is confronted with a world that says he isn't enough, he is reminded he always matters.

VERA'S VIEW

One reason why I have been so excited to write this book is that I get to share so many titles that I wish I'd had the chance to read as a young child. I *wish* a teacher would have read *All Because You Matter* to me as I sat in a class as the only child of color. My wish for non-BIPOC educators is that they realize that not only do children of color need this story, but white children need this story, too.

START SMALL

Opening pages (double spread)

What does it mean to matter? Write or draw a list of all the ways you matter.

BE CONSISTENT

And just like moons… (double spread)

What do you think the young girl is thinking? The words say, "and the whispers and giggles begin," followed by, "What kind of name is that?"

Why is it important to pronounce someone's name correctly? How are our names part of our identity?

Or the time you'll see... **(double spread)**

Have you ever studied hard for a test or project but got the answers wrong? What do you notice about the little boy and his work?

KEEP CONSTANT

The Black Lives Matter Foundation is an organized movement advocating for non-violent civil disobedience in protest against incidents of police brutality against African American (Black) people. Racism is the belief that one person is better than another person because of their skin color. People who are racist or commit racist acts are trying to cause physical, financial, mental, and/or emotional harm. Of course, all lives matter. However, right now, Black men, women, and sometimes children are victims of police violence at a higher rate than other people. So it's important that right now we do all we can to end racism and injustice against all Black people. Imagine you are outside playing with a group of friends. While you are playing, you fall down and scrape your knee. Should we give everyone a band-age because everyone matters, or should we just give you the bandage because right now you need it more than everyone else? We should give you the bandage right now so that you can heal. The rest of your friends are OK at the moment and can support you until you are better and ready to play in the same way they can. This is why Black lives matter.

LET'S MAKE A PLAN OF ACTION

- What are ways you can make sure Black lives matter?
- How can you use your voice, art, writing, or anything you want to speak out and take action against racism?
- What does your school do to show that it is antiracist and that Black lives matter?

Because I read this book, I now know _____ .

Because I read this book, I wonder _____ .

Because I read this book, I understand _____ .

LEARNING FOR JUSTICE STANDARDS

Identity
Diversity
Justice
Action

ELA STANDARDS

- Students will ask and answer questions about key details in a text.

- Students will acknowledge differences in the points of view of characters.

- Students will describe how characters in a story respond to major events and challenges.

- Students will compare and contrast the adventures and experiences of characters in stories.

INTERSECTIONALLIES: WE MAKE ROOM FOR ALL

Written by Chelsea Johnson, LaToya Council, and Carolyn Choi
Illustrated by Ashley Seil Smith

BOOK BIOGRAPHY

Intersectionality is a term coined by Dr. Kimberlé Crenshaw. Intersectionality is the way that all parts of our identity show up in different parts of our lives. *IntersectionAllies* takes a look at a group of young children and how their individual identities are important. What is equally important is how they use their voice and actions to create inclusive spaces for each other.

VERA'S VIEW

One of the best components of this book is the extensive back matter. It includes definitions, book recommendations, author biographies, and more. *IntersectionAllies* is a book I continue to reference when working with educators who are looking for a way to engage younger learners in conversations around identity.

START SMALL

Opening pages (double spread)

How are you similar to or different from your group of friends?

BE CONSISTENT

The clothes that you wear… **(double spread)**

How can clothes be an expression of our identity? Are there certain types of clothing you want to learn more about?

Race, religion, citizenship… **(pages)**

How is life different for you than for a friend?

KEEP CONSTANT

Each of our identities is important and impacts how we experience the world. When you have a friend who has multiple identities that are different from your own, they may have different privileges and experiences than you. It's important to understand the different identities of people so that you can be an ally. An ally is someone who stands with you even if your identities are different. An ally uses their voice and privilege to speak up against injustice.

Let's Make a Plan of Action

- Have you ever stood up for a friend? What can you say or do when you see a friend who is being treated unfairly?
- What are some things you believe in speaking up about?
- How do you use your voice to make a difference?

Because I read this book, I now know _____ .

Because I read this book, I wonder _____ .

Because I read this book, I understand _____ .

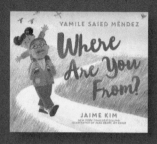

LEARNING FOR JUSTICE STANDARDS

Identity
Diversity

ELA STANDARDS

- Students will ask and answer questions about key details in a text.

- Students will acknowledge differences in the points of view of characters.

- Students will compare and contrast the adventures and experiences of characters in stories.

- Students will describe how characters in a story respond to major events and challenges.

WHERE ARE YOU FROM?

Written by Yamile Saied Méndez
Illustrated by Jaime Kim

BOOK BIOGRAPHY

Where Are You From? is the story of a young girl discovering her identity. People outside of her family are constantly asking her where she is from in an effort to understand what they perceive her identity to be. After a conversation with her grandfather, the young girl has a stronger understanding of exactly where she is from.

VERA'S VIEW

Where are you from? is a question often asked as people try to determine a person's identity. This question can often be well meaning, but the impact can be quite harmful. This story is such a beautiful reminder that if you don't know your family's ancestry, you are from the love and connectedness of your family.

START SMALL

Opening pages (double spread)

What would you say if someone asked you, "Where are you from?"

BE CONSISTENT

From this land… (double spread)

An ancestor is someone in your family from long ago. When someone uses the word *ancestor*, they usually mean someone like a great-great-great-great-great-grandparent. On these pages, the grandfather is describing the place where the girl's ancestors came from. He says the ancestors "were in chains because of the color of their skin." What do you think that could mean? What do you know about history that would help you understand these pages?

He points to his heart… (pages)

The girl wants her grandfather to give her the name of the place she is from. Her grandfather responds by pointing to his heart. He says she is from "my love and the love of all those before us." How does the love of family help contribute to someone's understanding of their identity?

KEEP CONSTANT

Let's talk about intent versus impact. Sometimes when we are curious, we may ask questions or say something that is offensive and causes a negative impact on the other person. You may not have *intended* to offend someone with your questions, but the *impact* was that what you said caused harm. It's important to apologize and check in with someone if you unintentionally caused harm with your question.

LET'S MAKE A PLAN OF ACTION

- What is another way you can ask someone where they are from that makes sure they feel included?
- Sometimes, people ask where someone is from in an effort to make them feel like they don't belong. What can you say or do when you hear someone ask another person where they are from?
- Remember what we talked about with intent versus impact. Can you think of some ways you may have meant to do something nice or right, but the impact was harmful or hurtful? How can you help repair the hurt you may have caused?

Because I read this book, I now know _____ .

Because I read this book, I wonder _____ .

Because I read this book, I understand _____ .

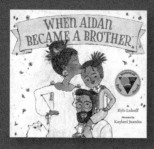

LEARNING FOR
JUSTICE STANDARDS

Identity
Diversity
Justice
Action

ELA STANDARDS

- Students will ask and answer questions about key details in a text.

- Students will acknowledge differences in the points of view of characters.

- Students will compare and contrast the adventures and experiences of characters in stories.

- Students will describe how characters in a story respond to major events and challenges.

WHEN AIDAN BECAME A BROTHER

Written by Kyle Lukoff
Illustrated by Kaylani Juanita

BOOK BIOGRAPHY

At Aidan's birth, everyone thought he was a girl. As Aidan grew older, he realized that he wasn't a girl and was a trans boy. Through lots of conversations and research and help, Aidan and his parents made sure that Aidan's heart, mind, and body were happy. Soon, his mother and father tell Aidan that they are having another baby and Aidan will become a big brother. Aidan wants to be sure everything is "just right" for his sibling.

VERA'S VIEW

I can't wait until libraries around the world are overflowing with beautiful stories like this one. I am constantly referencing this story to help myself be a better ally and advocate. What a powerful message to transgender (and all) children about the importance of being honest and open with your family. This is an important story about advocating for your feelings even if you don't have all the information to explain exactly how you feel.

START SMALL

Opening pages (double spread)

The illustrator did amazing work in expressing Aidan's emotions in the opening pages. Look around the room. What evidence can you find that Aiden is unhappy?

BE CONSISTENT

It was hard to tell his parents… (page)

Why was it harder for Aidan not to tell his parents about his identity?

The author says, "They learned a lot from other families with transgender kids." What does it mean for a person to be transgender?

Then one day… (page)

Aidan wants to be sure his sibling feels understood right away. Why does Aidan want that experience for his sibling? What are some ways you help people understand your identity?

KEEP CONSTANT

Someone is transgender if their gender identity is different from the gender their family or other adults thought they were at birth. People who identify as cisgender have a gender identity that matches the gender they were assigned at birth. There are many other ways that gender identity can be expressed or identified.

LET'S MAKE A PLAN OF ACTION

- How does the way you express your gender help confirm your identity?
- What can we do if we see someone who is transgender be made fun of? How can we be sure everyone feels included in our classroom?
- Let's think about the language we are using. Are we ensuring everyone feels included (e.g., not saying boy/girl colors or clothes)? How can we change our language to be more inclusive?

Because I read this book, I now know _____ .

Because I read this book, I wonder _____ .

Because I read this book, I understand _____ .

TEACHER TALK

FEATURED EDUCATOR: Asmahan Mashrah

Dearborn, Michigan. Fourth grade, self-contained classroom. Seven years in education. BIPOC educator—the global majority—and non-Christian. Pronouns: she/her.

VERA: Can you talk to me a bit about your experience with teaching "controversial" topics through read alouds?

ASMAHAN: Overall, I have had positive responses from students and parents. Usually, upper elementary students are thrilled to see us reading picture books. Sometimes the misconception is picture books are for lower grades, but that is far from the truth. In my classroom, picture books have allowed my students to engage in critical and thoughtful conversations around a variety of topics. We have discussed holidays around the world from various faiths, families and how they can look different than others, homelessness, poverty, race, and much more. Having picture books has allowed my students to dig deep into their learning, has kept them engaged and excited. Many students were able to identify themselves in these books and share about their connections with the various topics. Sharing "controversial" topics has allowed our classroom to really build a strong foundation and relationships.

VERA: What are some challenges you've faced?

ASMAHAN: I have faced challenges in regard to sharing holidays of various faiths other than the Christian faith. When discussing Eid/Ramadan, I received pushback from parents on why these holidays were being discussed in the classroom and what my intentions were. I was accused of indoctrination, which is mind-boggling. We had to have a huge discussion with the administration, and I was supported by my administration but also made it clear to the parents that in our classroom, holidays from various faiths were included and it was linked to standards of social-emotional learning and our geography unit. I also informed the parent

that they never discussed any issues before Eid/Ramadan, and all the students were exposed to Christian holidays, Jewish holidays, Hindu holidays, along with Muslim holidays. One group of people's holiday wasn't favored or pushed in favor of another. Afterward, the parent did apologize, but the damage was done.

VERA: Why is the work of integrating "controversial" books into your daily read-aloud schedule important or meaningful to you?

ASMAHAN: Integrating these topics is important because they build foundations for empathetic human beings. I may never know what the students' experience or lack thereof is, and therefore providing opportunities for students to learn, talk, critique, and grow in a safe space will allow them to harness their critical thinking skills for use in the future. It will also provide them with a background for addressing certain people or situations in a caring and humane manner, and so that is why it's so important for us to make sure that we are providing a space for learners to explore and question.

VERA: What have you noticed in your students/children as a result of rebellious read alouds?

ASMAHAN: My students have grown immensely throughout the year. They are more eager to question things with a critical lens, they are more compassionate and empathetic, they are more excited to make connections and learn from others.

VERA: What is one tip or piece of advice you would give to educators?

ASMAHAN: Provide experiences for students to see themselves and others in. Picture books will allow you to do that. Be intentional in the books you are sharing based on your student demographic and their interests, have meaningful discussions that are

student-led, and encourage respectful disagreements and conversations.

VERA: What are your top five favorite read alouds?

ASMAHAN:

- *Ramadan Moon* by Na'ima B. Robert
- *Under My Hijab* by Hena Khan
- *I Am Human* by Susan Verde
- *All Because You Matter* by Tami Charles
- *Your Name Is a Song* by Jamilah Thompkins-Bigelow
- *In My Mosque (Masjid)* by M. O. Yuksel

LEARNING FOR JUSTICE STANDARDS

Identity
Diversity
Justice
Action

ELA STANDARDS

- Students will ask and answer questions about key details in a text.

- Students will acknowledge differences in the points of view of characters.

- Students will describe how characters in a story respond to major events and challenges.

- Students will compare and contrast the adventures and experiences of characters in stories.

Conversations around disabilities is an area in which I feel like I have so much more learning to do. Perhaps you feel the same. However, I am trying to follow and interact with creators and educators who are disabled and to share their perspectives and education with an audience. The books in this unit invite students to ask questions instead of promoting silence or shame.

ALL THE WAY TO THE TOP

How One Girl's Fight for Americans With Disabilities Changed Everything

Written by Annette Bay Pimentel
Illustrated by Nabi H. Ali

BOOK BIOGRAPHY

All the Way to the Top is the true story of Jennifer Keelan's fight for accessibility for people with disabilities. Jennifer consistently faced accessibility obstacles and knew not only was it unfair, but it was also inequitable. *All the Way to the Top* is the story of Jennifer's fight for equality.

VERA'S VIEW

This is one of those eye-opening-moments type of books. I read through all of Jennifer's experiences and recognized how much nondisabled privilege I have. Did you know that Congress initially believed the Americans with Disabilities Act would be too expensive and difficult to implement?

START SMALL

The school's not far… (double spread)

How do you get to school each day? Are there any obstacles for you on your way to school?

BE CONSISTENT

Her Grandpa eases her wheelchair… (page)

A disability is a physical or mental condition that limits a person's movements, senses, or abilities. Not all disabilities can be seen.

Do you think it's fair that people with disabilities did not have equitable access to buildings, schools, or even sidewalks? How do you think people with disabilities felt about this? What are some of the ways spaces could be made more accessible?

Jennifer and her family… (pages)

A protest is when a group of people gather together to use their voices and speak up for what they believe in. What is something you feel strongly about? How do you use your voice to speak up?

She slides out of her wheelchair… (double spread)

How do you think Jennifer felt at this moment? Why was it important for her to do this? Can you think of other people throughout history who have protested for change for the better?

KEEP CONSTANT

The Americans with Disabilities Act was passed in 1990. There are still many ways in which people with disabilities do not have access to spaces or opportunities in the same way that nondisabled people do. We must continue to advocate and work toward ensuring that all spaces are inclusive and equitable.

LET'S MAKE A PLAN OF ACTION

- What are the ways in which your school is inclusive and accessible? What are the ways in which it is not?
- How can nondisabled people be allies to people with disabilities?
- Have you been to a protest before? What would you protest for and why?

Because I read this book, I now know _____.

Because I read this book, I wonder _____.

Because I read this book, I understand _____.

OUR DISABILITIES ARE IMPORTANT

LEARNING FOR JUSTICE STANDARDS

Identity
Diversity

ELA STANDARDS

- Students will ask and answer questions about key details in a text.

- Students will acknowledge differences in the points of view of characters.

- Students will describe how characters in a story respond to major events and challenges.

- Students will compare and contrast the adventures and experiences of characters in stories.

▶ THE REMEMBER BALLOONS

Written by Jessie Oliveros
Illustrated by Dana Wulfekotte

BOOK BIOGRAPHY

The Remember Balloons is a story about how a little boy and his grandpa remember the special memories they have shared together. However, the grandfather is struggling with Alzheimer's/dementia and is losing his memory. *The Remember Balloons* is a beautiful explanation of the anger, sadness, fear, and hope family members go through while witnessing their loved ones lose their memories.

VERA'S VIEW

Before my Papa passed, he (and my family) lived through his struggles with dementia. The thought of losing memories is terrifyingly sad. I can't imagine what he must have felt as he struggled to hold on to the things that seemed so lucid to me. I cried as I read this book the first time. I was reminded of my Papa (the grandfather in the story even looks like mine), and I was encouraged to remember that I can hold on to the balloons of my memories with him.

START SMALL

This one's my favorite… (double spread)

What is one of your most favorite memories?

BE CONSISTENT

but grandpa has been having problems... (double spread)

Dementia is a term for losing memory, language, or problem-solving abilities that often happens in elderly people. James's grandfather is suffering with memory loss. How do James and his family feel about the memory loss? How would you help someone who is losing their memory?

Why did you let it go? (pages)

What do you notice about the way James is speaking to his grandfather? When his grandfather goes to comfort him, James notices that he doesn't "ruffle my hair like he always did." What is happening to his grandfather's memory? How is that affecting his relationship with James and the rest of the family?

KEEP CONSTANT

As family needs change and there are more multigenerational families residing in one home than ever before, children need to have conversations about the changes they might notice in their older family members. Having open and honest conversations around what is happening or what will happen to our families as they age helps children have ownership of their emotions and understanding of how they can play a part in helping the family structure be successful and healthy.

LET'S MAKE A PLAN OF ACTION

- How do you express yourself when you are feeling mad or angry at a family member? How can you help that family member understand your feelings?

- How can you record or save memories that are important to you, your family, or your community? How can you share those memories with others?

- How does your community take care of people as they get older? What ideas do you have to make sure older people are taken care of?

Because I read this book, I now know _____ .

Because I read this book, I wonder _____ .

Because I read this book, I understand _____ .

LEARNING FOR JUSTICE STANDARDS

Identity
Diversity
Justice
Action

ELA STANDARDS

- Students will ask and answer questions about key details in a text.

- Students will acknowledge differences in the points of view of characters.

- Students will describe how characters in a story respond to major events and challenges.

- Students will compare and contrast the adventures and experiences of characters in stories.

WE WANT TO GO TO SCHOOL

Written by Maryann Cocca-Leffler and Janine Leffler

BOOK BIOGRAPHY

We Want to Go to School is the story of the landmark legal case *Mills v. Board of Education of the District of Columbia*. This case gave all children access to public education regardless of disability.

VERA'S VIEW

Reading this book reminded me of how much privilege I have. I had no idea that there was an actual court case that ensured disabled students could have access to public education. It was also incredibly eye-opening that it wasn't until 1990 that the Americans with Disabilities Act was signed into law. The act prohibits discrimination against individuals with disabilities in areas of public life.

START SMALL

So when I was three (double spread)

Who is your teacher? Do you have more than one teacher? What do your teachers help you do?

BE CONSISTENT

It is the same way for other kids… (page)

A disability is a physical or mental condition that limits a person's movements, senses, or abilities. Not all disabilities can be seen.

Do you think it's fair that children with disabilities were not allowed to attend public school? How would you react if you were told you couldn't attend school because of who you are? What could you do to make a change?

Sometimes, children with disabilities were… (pages)

Segregated means to keep separate from something else. We have learned and talked about segregation before. When we talked about segregation before, it was in reference to race. How is this type of segregation similar to or different from the segregation we learned about earlier?

But in 1971… (double spread)

What do you notice about the children who said, "No! This isn't right"?

What other types of discrimination could these children have faced?

What would you have done if you were a student at a school that wouldn't allow students with disabilities to attend?

KEEP CONSTANT

At times it can feel uncomfortable for nondisabled people to have conversations around disabilities. It's important to be sure to research and use correct and up-to-date terminology when discussing the ways that ableism prevents various areas of daily life from being completely accessible to all.

LET'S MAKE A PLAN OF ACTION

- Take a walk around your school. In what ways is your school set up to be inclusive of every student?
- What things would you need to change at your school or in your community for there to be more inclusivity?
- How can you help make sure that every student in your classroom or at your school feels welcome and included?

Because I read this book, I now know _____.

Because I read this book, I wonder _____.

Because I read this book, I understand _____.

OUR DISABILITIES ARE IMPORTANT

LEARNING FOR JUSTICE STANDARDS

Identity
Diversity
Justice
Action

ELA STANDARDS

- Students will ask and answer questions about key details in a text.

- Students will acknowledge differences in the points of view of characters.

- Students will compare and contrast the adventures and experiences of characters in stories.

- Students will describe how characters in a story respond to major events and challenges.

AWESOMELY EMMA: A CHARLEY AND EMMA STORY

Written by Amy Webb
Illustrated by Merrilee Liddiard

BOOK BIOGRAPHY

Emma has limb differences. She loves creating art, playing with her friends, and learning in school. One day her class is going to take a field trip to the art museum. When they arrive, Emma is disappointed to find that there is no front entrance for people who use a wheelchair. Emma must enter the museum from the back. Despite this, Emma enjoys her time at the museum—that is, until her friend Charley oversteps Emma's boundary.

VERA'S VIEW

Great children's books that feature a child with a visible disability have been hard for me to find. What I love about this book is the multiple talking points to engage children in conversations around disability, consent, advocacy, and equality.

START SMALL

Opening pages (double spread)

What is something you love to do? How does it make you feel when you are doing what you love to do?

BE CONSISTENT

When they got to the museum… (page)

What is inequitable about the ramp not being in the front of the building? What does this mean for people who use wheelchairs or other adaptive devices? What does this mean for people who do not use wheelchairs?

Suddenly Charley grabbed… (double spread)

Charley is trying to help Emma do different things, but Emma does not seem happy. Why do you think Emma is unhappy? Have there been times when you overstepped?

Emma looked at her sketchpad… (page)

Why was it important that Emma write the letter to the art museum?

Has there been a time when you've spoken up for change?

KEEP CONSTANT

There is nothing wrong with having a disability. Disabilities can be visible or invisible. Having a disability just means you may do things in a different way from other people. People with disabilities are not helpless.

LET'S MAKE A PLAN OF ACTION

- Is your school accessible to all bodies? What can you do to help make your school more accessible?
- What can you do if you notice a place isn't accessible for everyone?
- What are some ways you can ask for consent before helping someone?

Because I read this book, I now know _____ .

Because I read this book, I wonder _____ .

Because I read this book, I understand _____ .

OUR DISABILITIES ARE IMPORTANT

LEARNING FOR JUSTICE STANDARDS

Identity
Diversity
Justice
Action

ELA STANDARDS

- Students will ask and answer questions about key details in a text.

- Students will acknowledge differences in the points of view of characters.

- Students will compare and contrast the adventures and experiences of characters in stories.

- Students will describe how characters in a story respond to major events and challenges.

I TALK LIKE A RIVER

Written by Jordan Scott
Illustrated by Sydney Smith

BOOK BIOGRAPHY

I Talk Like a River is an emotional journey of a little boy who speaks with a stutter. After the boy has a tough speech day, his father takes him somewhere quiet. While sitting on the bank of the river together, the father compares the child's speech to water in the river, "bubbling, whirling, churning, and crashing."

VERA'S VIEW

Speaking with a stutter is a common speech disorder. In fact, our forty-sixth president, Joe Biden, has been open about his experiences with speaking with a stutter. It's important for students to be aware that there are many disabilities that are not immediately visible.

START SMALL

Opening pages (double spread)

What are some sounds you hear when you first wake up? What are some of the things you say when you first wake up?

BE CONSISTENT

The P in pine tree… (page)

A stutter (sometimes called stammer) is a speech disorder that involves the fluency or flow of speech. How do you think the character feels about his stutter?

At school, I hide in the back… (double spread)

The boy doesn't want to talk in front of his classmates because of his stutter. How could the teacher be more accommodating of this student's feelings? What would you have done or said if you were in the class?

I feel a storm in my belly… (page)

The boy is overcome with emotions. How do you think he is feeling? Have you ever felt a storm in your belly? What do you think the boy needs to feel better?

KEEP CONSTANT

Disabilities can be visible or invisible. Having a disability just means you may do things in a different way from other people. Sometimes, people without a disability can feel like they want to "fix" someone's disability. Instead, it's important to be patient, listen, and learn how to be supportive.

LET'S MAKE A PLAN OF ACTION

- What can we do if we hear a classmate laughing at another student for the way they speak?
- How do you find ways to accept or understand the ways that you are different?
- In what ways can we support other students who have a learning or physical disability without taking over for them?

Because I read this book, I now know _____ .

Because I read this book, I wonder _____ .

Because I read this book, I understand _____ .

OUR DISABILITIES ARE IMPORTANT

TEACHER TALK

FEATURED EDUCATOR: Amanda Culver

Victoria, British Columbia, on the traditional lands of the Esquimalt and Songhees Nations. First grade French immersion. Ten years in education. Nonbinary educator. Pronouns: she/they. (View this video interview on the online companion, resources.corwin.com/rebellious.)

VERA: Can you talk to me a bit about your experience with teaching "controversial" topics through read alouds?

AMANDA: So, when I first started teaching, I was a high school teacher, and read alouds weren't really a part of anything I purposely did. And now looking back, I was like, "Oh my gosh. I wish I had included more while I was teaching high school." And especially some of these controversial topics, they never necessarily came up, which is ridiculous because I also taught ancient history, and I think it was just from me being so uninformed as an educator and as a person. I didn't know really what I was doing in terms of bringing controversial stuff into the classroom, and it was more so through extracurriculars where I started to find my ground with like, "Oh, OK. These are controversial topics. I need to talk about these with my students." And when I moved provinces is when I switched grade levels.

So, I went from high school down to grade four or five. And part of the curriculum in B.C. [British Columbia] is talking about truth and reconciliation and Indigenous peoples, and that's really my students' first experience learning about what's going on with our history. And because I didn't know so much—really anything—about it, it was more learning for me before I could do a good job of sharing it with them. But then I also realized my students don't know anything about the 2SLGBTQIA+ community, and they don't know about racism and again, these controversial topics. So, when I first moved out here, it was a huge jump from the high school to grade four/five. And I was just figuring out what on earth am I doing in the classroom period, but that's also where I started to bring in these topics

through read alouds and I got some pushback, and I think that's one of the questions later, so I can save more of that for then.

But that's where I started to explore what read alouds were available to bring in these heavier topics with my students, and I noticed our library space didn't really have many options available either. I was like, "Well, if I'm going to spend money on my classroom, it's going to be on books." So, this is just a little sample, but yeah, so that's really where my experience started. And then after that year of teaching grade four/five is when I moved down to grade one and I was like, "Hey, these are foundational years." This is a really important time to start introducing these topics where students are still feeling safe to ask those questions because they don't necessarily know that they're controversial. It was perfect bringing a read aloud every single day, and anywhere I can bring in these controversial topics I was.

And this past year, we were in person the full year and I was able to do a read aloud all 174 days that we were in person, and I feel like the majority of them were controversial topics. And by the end of the year, my students were able to have conversations amongst themselves and with their families without that fear of, "Am I going to say or do the wrong thing?" So, this past year really helped me build that confidence of the texts I'm choosing to bring into my space so that I can share it with other teachers as well, like, "Here's some resources. Please, please, please bring this into your space. I'll come and do a read aloud for your class just to show you what it looks like, because these conversations, they need to be happening. When you look at what's going on in the world, there's no way that we

OUR DISABILITIES ARE IMPORTANT

can justify staying silent." So, yeah, that's really where my journey with these read alouds has been, is from absolutely nothing and knowing nothing to being a book pusher and trying to really get it to my students, to the families as much as I could.

VERA: I love that and I love that there is a vulnerability, I think, that educators have trouble with not knowing because we're supposed to be—and I talked about this yesterday with another interviewee—we're supposed to be, or this ancient idea, that teachers are this vessel that disperses this knowledge. And when we let that go and accept the fact that we don't know so much, then we can use the read alouds as a medium for both the reader and the student to let this be an opportunity to be like, "Did you know that this is happening, this happened? I didn't know that. Let's read about it. What questions do we have about it?" And I think if we can use read alouds to break the vulnerability for ourselves, it just has a double impact because, of course, the children will be excited to engage in it, but then it gives you the freedom to be OK with being ignorant and not in a terrible way. Being ignorant about a subject matter is how we rely on books and information to help us move past that.

AMANDA: Yeah. And I think having a picture book as a suggestion to families as, "Here's what we did in class. Here's the book that we read if you want to continue those conversations at home. Go find a book and I'm giving you the suggestions to do so, too."

VERA: What are some challenges you've faced?

AMANDA: Well, I think the first place of pushback really came from myself and my own upbringing. And I grew up in a Catholic family and being from a mixed background as well, there's a lot of racism that I experienced within my own family or resolved with my own family, and it was just these mindsets that have to change or hear before I could move forward. And even as a queer educator, there was so much homophobia that I was self-imposing as well, so there's just those sorts of challenges, fighting

myself so that I can do better. And then within the classroom space, there were of course families that were very, like, "Well, we don't believe this at home, so you shouldn't be teaching it in the classroom." And a great thing about teaching in B.C. is that we do have the curriculum to back us up with what we can share with families, so it really helps having policies and procedures in place that support this learning.

Some of the initial pushback with teaching grade four/five class and not having resources in the library was the person making the purchasing decisions decided that, "Well, this isn't worth spending our money on because it's in the past. It's not a present issue," right? So, there was a lot of those sorts of feelings that existed within the school I was in. And so trying to move forward through, it was always a tipping point. Even though I had curriculum to support me, it wasn't necessarily there with the staff. And in the past couple of years, I've been our school SOGI rep, which is sexual orientation, gender identity. So, I've been the rep for our school and so I'm bringing these resources in, but there's also been a lot of pushback of, like, "Well, we don't want to do this because what will the parents think or what will the families think?"

And I think that's really the biggest shift that needs to happen is the school side as well. So, I know these are important issues. We have curriculum to support us, we have policies to support us, so what's really stopping us? And that's where I think it comes back to those internalized beliefs that need to be challenged. And it's scary and uncomfortable, but it's important to do, so I think that's more so where a lot of it comes from. I have had parents push back and say, like, "We don't want you reading this or talking about this, because it goes against what we believe at home." My sassy response wants to be like, "Well, we're at school. School is not home. You can teach what you want to at home, but this is school and it's a public school, and this is our curriculum and here's the policy."

So, it always comes back to that legal language, I guess, that helps, I guess, calm down the family side

Our Disabilities Are Important ● 107

of things, and having supportive admin helps as well. I've been in cases where the admin haven't been supportive. And as a queer educator, I couldn't justify staying in those spaces either. If I'm not going to have admin support, then I'm not going to feel comfortable myself in the classroom.

VERA: Why is the work of integrating "controversial" books into your daily read-aloud schedule important or meaningful to you?

AMANDA: Well, I think almost everyone is familiar with the idea of books are windows and they opened doors like…just that idea in general. But I think especially when we look and we're thinking, we're trying to prepare these little people to be big people in the world outside. And when we look at the world outside, these are the things that we're seeing and these are things that maybe you don't believe at home, but they exist in the world. So, I think just using them as opportunities to bring the world into the classroom in more kid-friendly ways and I think even in less intimidating ways. I've used picture books with my own family too and say, like, "Hey, these are some issues in a more, I guess, palatable format. So, let's bring that in before we dive deeper into the deeper learning and the harder conversations."

VERA: What have you noticed in your students as a result of rebellious read alouds?

AMANDA: I think part of me is just so excited to hear the conversations they're having with themselves. One of the big things that we focused on this past year was not assuming a character's gender unless we are told. And so closer to the end of the year and after doing these read alouds every single day, students were correcting me. So, I would pull out a book and it was a book where I already knew the character's gender, so I used the pronoun *she* and *her* and students were like, "But they haven't told us yet, so how do you know?" I was like, "Wow. Great question. Thank you for stopping me." So, it seemed like these six- and seven-year-olds are feeling comfortable enough to interrupt me like an adult who's

been sharing all this with them, and also they're having conversations at home. We talked about how we got some pushback from families, but we also get a lot of support and just the general support from families too.

I've had some parents come and say, "We were reading this book and my child stopped me and said, 'Well, we don't know what pronouns they use, so we need to wait and see.'" So, just knowing that this is extending beyond the 15 minutes we're doing in class and reading a book is something that just fills my educator heart. Yeah, so that's super exciting to see. It's what motivates me to continue to bring these resources into the classroom and also to encourage other teachers to bring them in as well. We are seeing these little changes with these little people, which is super exciting.

VERA: And that specific lesson about waiting until you know is a big lesson. It's a small something you bring about in a book, and we can always rely on stories to provide that lesson as an opportunity, but that's a big life lesson. And I think it's so powerful that you've helped your students be able to say, "I don't know, so I'm not going to make an assumption. And I'm going to wait until I have more information until I can apply what I know to what they identify as, to be able to move along." And it's without judgment, and it's without, I think, some of the bigger adult feelings we put on gender identity and pronouns. That is going to be a huge shift. I think of when we worked with itty-bitties, that when they become older and I think more self-realized in their teenage years, how important it will be for any of them whose gender might not be what they were assigned at birth to be able to be like, "My teacher recognized that that lesson was important enough at six and seven." It's huge. It's so huge.

VERA: What is one tip or piece of advice you would give to educators?

AMANDA: I think just jump right in. I think a huge thing that held me back was just knowing that I didn't know, and being afraid to mess up or being afraid to say the wrong thing, and knowing that my opinions can change too. So, I think just taking that leap, jump right in, see where the conversations head. You can learn more together as well. It's OK to say, "I don't know." I think just jumping in is a huge, huge, huge first step. It's not as scary. It can be uncomfortable, but it's not as scary.

VERA: What are your top five favorite read alouds?

AMANDA: So, this is the one that I had to do a bit of prep for because I was like, "I don't know how to pick." And then I figured, "Well, as a queer educator, maybe I'll just pick both from my queer resources or the books that have my little rainbow tape on the spines and I'll pick from there." So, I tried to grab ones that were available in French and English on Bookwell, so I have five in front of me, so I'll share those.

The first one, the English title is *Julián Is a Mermaid* [by Jessica Love], classic. This one, I think, has a lot of really cool conversations to the classroom with the gender stereotypes that students were making, but I think also my favorite page is really when you open the first cover and you have various body sizes. That's hugely missing from picture books, so that one's definitely one of my favorites.

Another one which is available in French is *A Day in the Life of Marlon Bundo* [by Jill Twiss]. It's so funny, but there's a lot of political things hidden within this book that open up the opportunity to have further discussions, so this one is a favorite as well.

Prince and Knight [by Daniel Haack] is one that students are always surprised by, like, "Wait, what's going on?" And then this is one that they've often asked me to read over and over, so it's a student favorite, so it has to be teacher favorite.

VERA: I think that my kids are so….My kids have ripped that book because they have loved it so much, and maybe it's because the narrative of the fairy tale is so ingrained in us that this one is so not that, that they're obsessed with that story in a beautiful way. They're just like, "What are you…." There's

adventure, but there's this romance, and it's one of my favorite because it's their favorite book.

AMANDA: When they learn that there is a second one as well, *Maiden and Princess* [by Daniel Haack], they're like, "Can you read that one?" I'm like, "Well, it's not available in French, but yes, I will read that one to you for sure." So, this is one I have multiple copies of in my classroom as well.

A more recent one is by a local author, so we use that to make some connections too, it's *Pride Puppy!* [by Robin Stevenson]. And this one, it's lovely because there's so many pictures that invite conversation about a lot of different elements of the queer community. There's the page that has the two-spirit flag, and so that brings in conversation to our students where, like, "Well, we've seen this before, so what is it?" And so it's lovely. It's one of our favorites, it's the newer one.

And then the last one I had to choose was by a non-binary author and brings in a lot of topics about pronouns as well. And I try to bring in books that have people as the main characters, but this one, my students love this type of character too. It's *Peanut Goes for the Gold* [by Jonathan Van Ness]. I had one student that's like, "Hey, I know Jonathan Van Ness. We watched *Queer Eye* at home. I was like, "Oh, you do?" So there was instant connection. Those were the five that I chose for my large selection.

VERA: No one has said any of those, so I love that there's this like….You expect people to have different opinions, but I love that everyone [I've interviewed] has top fives that are completely different for various reasons. That was my last question, but I'd love to talk to you about anything on your mind or something that you want, you feel like wasn't answered or something you want to add.

AMANDA: So, again, I'm just super thankful for the opportunity to have this conversation. One, I love books, and so that's what pushed me to reach out to you as well. And also thanks for creating the space for all of us. It's important work, and even if it gets one more teacher on this journey, then it's all worth it.

OUR DISABILITIES ARE IMPORTANT

VERA: Exactly. Yeah, thank you so much. I really feel like, again, really having a perspective of the same thing helps educators feel more confident in the fact that you are on the right track. Like you said, if you're feeling nervous or scared, just jumping in, that validation really needs to be heard and my voice is not the only voice who needs to say that. So, I'm trying to limit how many people I interview, but I want to interview so many people because it's just so (a) interesting, but (b) it's like you said, important work that I think really—especially during what we're going through now globally—we just really need to hear that we all need to do better and do a bit more, and it can be as easy as a read aloud.

Notes from Classroom Conversations About Disabilities

OUR FOODS ARE IMPORTANT

LEARNING FOR JUSTICE STANDARDS

Identity
Diversity

ELA STANDARDS

- Students will ask and answer questions about key details in a text.

- Students will acknowledge differences in the points of view of characters.

Food! The universal uniter! I love this unit! Mostly because the books in this unit make my mouth water. But also because these books show the power of food. The books featured in this unit showcase the different ways food brings friends and family together, tells a culture's history, or can encourage and inspire change and innovation. Be sure to keep a napkin ready as you might find yourself drooling throughout these read alouds.

TOMATOES FOR NEELA

Written by Padma Lakshmi
Illustrated by Juana Martinez-Neal

BOOK BIOGRAPHY

Neela and her Amma love cooking together. In this story, they gather ingredients to make their Paati's favorite tomato sauce. In this story we learn a quick history of the origin of the word *tomato* and the importance the popular small fruit has for a family.

VERA'S VIEW

This story is written by Padma Lakshmi. I've watched her for years on the show *Top Chef*. She has a profound love for food, but what I truly admire about Padma is her advocacy for equality and justice. *Tomatoes for Neela* is an ode to Padma's family and their love and passion for food, but it also shares the importance and history tomatoes have had in our lives.

START SMALL

Opening pages (double spread)

What types of foods do you like to cook with your family? If you don't like to cook, what types of foods do you enjoy eating with your family?

BE CONSISTENT

Neela and her amma… (page)

Look at all the different types of foods on this page. Which of these foods are familiar to you? Which of these have you never heard of before? Would you try any of the unfamiliar foods?

But why can't we just buy… (double spread)

What do you notice about these pages?

Do you know who is in these pictures? How does understanding who these people are help us understand where our foods come from?

KEEP CONSTANT

Food is a way for people to connect with each other. We share food with one another as a sign of compassion. Recipes and food are sometimes passed down through generations. When we enjoy food with our friends and family, we sometimes don't think about where the ingredients come from. Farmworkers are the people who are responsible for bringing fresh fruits and vegetables to our stores. They often work long and hard for very little pay or basic rights like healthcare or safe working conditions.

LET'S MAKE A PLAN OF ACTION

- How can you help those who do not have access to fresh or healthy food choices?
- How can we learn more about where our food is grown or where it comes from? How could what we learn change what foods we eat or how we eat certain foods?
- How can we advocate for farmworkers like César Chávez or Dolores Huerta?

Because I read this book, I now know _____ .

Because I read this book, I wonder _____ .

Because I read this book, I understand _____ .

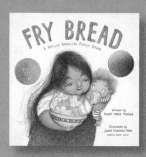

LEARNING FOR JUSTICE STANDARDS

Identity
Diversity

ELA STANDARDS

- Students will ask and answer questions about key details in a text.

- Students will acknowledge differences in the points of view of characters.

FRY BREAD

Written by Kevin Noble Maillard
Illustrated by Juana Martinez-Neal

BOOK BIOGRAPHY

Many families gather around food to connect and show they care for one another. Fry bread is a food shared in many Indigenous families. Created from simple ingredients, fry bread is rich in history.

VERA'S VIEW

I love food. I also love learning about (and tasting) new foods. *Fry Bread* is a beautiful story that shares the history, connection, and recipe for a traditional Indigenous food. I think most cultures have a bread (or bread-like food) that is included in their regular diet. The history or origin of the bread may be unknown or its story changed throughout history, yet its taste connects generations.

START SMALL

Opening pages (double spread)

What types of bread do you eat? What are some different types of breads you know of? Do you know how to make bread?

BE CONSISTENT

Fry bread is color… (page)

What do you notice about this page? Listen to the color words the author uses to describe the fry bread. What would be a color word you could use to describe your skin color?

Fry bread is history… (double spread)

What do you notice about these pages? How are they different from other pages in the book?

The author says, "The long walk, the stolen land, Strangers in our own world." If we know that the author and main characters are Indigenous people, what do these words mean for them? How does this change our understanding of fry bread?

KEEP CONSTANT

Food is a way for people to connect with each other. We share food with one another as a sign of compassion. Food and ingredients change based on location, diet, preference, and finances. Throughout history, oppressed people have had to change their food choices based on what was available to them in order to survive. Food deserts are places where it is difficult to find fresh or healthy food choices.

LET'S MAKE A PLAN OF ACTION

- What are the different ways foods bring your family/community together?
- How can food be used as a way to make change or bring about action?
- How can you help those who do not have access to fresh or healthy food choices?

Because I read this book, I now know _____ .

Because I read this book, I wonder _____ .

Because I read this book, I understand _____ .

LEARNING FOR JUSTICE STANDARDS

Identity
Diversity

ELA STANDARDS

- Students will ask and answer questions about key details in a text.

- Students will acknowledge differences in the points of view of characters.

- Students will describe how characters in a story respond to major events and challenges.

- Students will compare and contrast the adventures and experiences of characters in stories.

CHICKEN SOUP, CHICKEN SOUP

Written by Pamela Mayer
Illustrated by Deborah Melmon

BOOK BIOGRAPHY

Sophie has two grandmas. Grandma Ellie makes her chicken soup with kreplach. Grandma Nancy makes her chicken soup with wontons. Can Sophie show her grandmothers that even though their soups are very different, they are still very much the same?

VERA'S VIEW

I love this story because it gives a unique perspective on interracial families. *Chicken Soup, Chicken Soup* gives us a little insight into the perspective multiracial children have moving in between the different cultures, languages, and experiences that make up their family.

START SMALL

Opening pages (double spread)

What are some of your family traditions?

BE CONSISTENT

How could a piece of dough... (double spread)

Have you had chicken soup with kreplach before? Have you had chicken soup with wontons? What type of chicken soup do you eat with your family?

Presenting the first ever... (pages)

Sophie mixed the two soups together to create a new kind of soup. Sometimes, when two things are mixed together to create something new, it's called a *fusion*. Have you ever tried any fusion food before?

KEEP CONSTANT

Sophie found that while her grandmothers cook their soup in different ways, they actually have more in common than they thought. Our food comes from all over the country and sometimes the world. Food from different cultures is integrated into all of our lives. Think about your favorite foods. Are they from a different culture than your own? What culture or country do they originate from?

LET'S MAKE A PLAN OF ACTION

- How can you encourage friends and family to try new or different foods?
- How does your culture show up in the food you eat?
- In what ways does your family or culture keep memories of food? How can you keep those memories alive for others to learn from?

Because I read this book, I now know _____ .

Because I read this book, I wonder _____ .

Because I read this book, I understand _____ .

LEARNING FOR JUSTICE STANDARDS

Identity
Diversity

ELA STANDARDS

- Students will ask and answer questions about key details in a text.

- Students will acknowledge differences in the points of view of characters.

- Students will describe how characters in a story respond to major events and challenges.

- Students will compare and contrast the adventures and experiences of characters in stories.

BILAL COOKS DAAL

Written by Aisha Saeed
Illustrated by Anoosha Syed

BOOK BIOGRAPHY

Bilal is looking forward to helping his father make his favorite dish, daal. But what will his friends think of this yummy dish? Not only does daal take time to make, it is full of flavors and spices that Bilal's friends may not be familiar with. Although Bilal can't wait to share his food and culture with his friends, he's a bit nervous about what they'll think.

VERA'S VIEW

While I can be a picky eater, I'm not afraid to try new foods. I love this story because children love sharing their culture and food with their friends. Simultaneously, children are often honest about their opinions regarding smells and tastes they are unfamiliar with. This story can help encourage the idea of "not yucking someone's yum."

START SMALL

Opening pages (double spread)

What is one of your favorite meals?

BE CONSISTENT

It looks funny... (double spread)

Do you enjoy trying new foods? What do you do or say when you encounter a new food? What is a question you can ask about the food?

Is it ready?... (pages)

Calmly waiting for something is called having patience. What is something that was difficult for you to wait for?

KEEP CONSTANT

Food is an important way that cultures express themselves. Trying new or different food can be overwhelming. It's important to remember that what might be different looking or funny smelling to you may be delicious and important to someone else. When you are confronted with something that is different or unfamiliar, practice asking curious questions to learn more information.

LET'S MAKE A PLAN OF ACTION

- What is a curious question you can ask when you experience something different or unfamiliar?
- How can you let a friend know you care about or are interested in learning about their culture?
- How can you encourage friends and family to try new or different foods?

Because I read this book, I now know _____.

Because I read this book, I wonder _____.

Because I read this book, I understand _____.

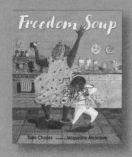

LEARNING FOR JUSTICE STANDARDS

Identity
Diversity

ELA STANDARDS

- Students will ask and answer questions about key details in a text.

- Students will acknowledge differences in the points of view of characters.

- Students will compare and contrast the adventures and experiences of characters in stories.

- Students will describe how characters in a story respond to major events and challenges.

FREEDOM SOUP

Written by Tami Charles
Illustrated by Jacqueline Alcántara

BOOK BIOGRAPHY

January 1, 1804, was Haitian Independence Day. A rebellion by enslaved people was the start of the Haitian Revolution, the most successful slave rebellion in the Western Hemisphere. Today on January 1, Haitians celebrate their fight for freedom and a new year with a delicious dish known as Freedom Soup.

VERA'S VIEW

I had never heard of Freedom Soup before reading this story. However, I do know the very long history of Black culture and food, like the stories of history told while cooking up chitlins or black-eyed peas. There is an extremely close connection between celebrations and food throughout different regions, ethnicities, cultures, and more.

START SMALL

Opening pages (double spread)

What foods or treats does your family make for holidays or celebrations?

BE CONSISTENT

Know why they call it... (double spread)

Ti Gran says, "Nothing in this world is free, not even freedom." What do you think she means by that? What does it mean for people to have freedom? What is it called when someone is denied their freedom? Can you think of examples in history when people have been denied their freedom?

I see the colors of freedom... (pages)

The Haitian people are now eating Freedom Soup. What has changed about their experience of eating and making Freedom Soup since before the revolution? Why might the Haitian people feel empowered at this moment?

Ti Gran lowers the flame... (pages)

Ti Gran says the tradition has been taught generation after generation. Why do you think the tradition of making Freedom Soup has been and continues to be passed down to each generation?

KEEP CONSTANT

When we say, "Our foods are important," it's not just because they are yummy or delicious. It is because often there is history tied to the foods we eat, especially those foods we eat during times of celebration. When we share our foods with people outside our culture, we want them to enjoy not only the taste but also the story that connects us to our culture.

LET'S MAKE A PLAN OF ACTION

- What can you learn about the history of enslaved people who lived where you live?
- How can you learn more about the foods you eat and the history of those foods?
- What can you learn about access to healthy foods based on the area you live in? What can you do to make healthy food more accessible in your area?

Because I read this book, I now know _____ .

Because I read this book, I wonder _____ .

Because I read this book, I understand _____ .

OUR FOODS ARE IMPORTANT

TEACHER TALK

FEATURED EDUCATOR: Danya Haber

New York, New York. Prekindergarten. Fourteen years in education, starting with secondary school, then elementary and now preschool. Non-Christian educator. Pronouns: she/her.

VERA: Can you talk to me a bit about your experience with teaching "controversial" topics through read alouds?

DANYA: Each year I try to introduce new concepts and ideas in my preschool classes. I do my best to make sure that we bring diversity of experience and a broader worldview than what might be represented in the classroom. A few years ago when Muslims were being bothered when they were praying in the streets, I showed my students videos of the Hajj in Mecca and what Muslim prayer looked like (in the context of our unit on travel, why people travel to Mecca, etc.) so that they would never be afraid if they saw a Muslim praying in public. We did not have any Muslims in our class, but it was important to me to be able to control their first exposure to something, to make sure that if down the line in their lives someone tried to paint Muslim prayer as "other" or "scary" they would know to push back. We have done the same thing with using singular *they* in a variety of books this year so that it becomes familiar to their ears, and if they ever hear that it's "too hard" or "not valid" they know at age four that it's totally doable and just another way to identify someone.

VERA: What are some challenges you've faced?

DANYA: The biggest pushbacks I have personally had in the classroom have been around gender, in particular allowing boys to dress up in what would typically be considered "girl" costumes. Parents have asked that we not allow it; we have had pushback about boys being "allowed" to wear makeup. Sometimes if we read a book about a gender-nonconforming character students might be confused, but in my experience they ask direct questions and are satisfied with the answer and explanation that "this is what makes this character feel most like themselves" or "just like you have clothes you like the best, this character does too." I try my best not to get into it with parents, and their beliefs do not have a role in my book choices or circle time conversations. If anything, knowing that some parents are still very firm along gender lines and roles motivates me to show my students the beautiful and broad gender spectrum because they are not getting that support and exposure at home.

VERA: Why is the work of integrating "controversial" books into your daily read-aloud schedule important or meaningful to you?

DANYA: Since I am teaching some of the youngest students that are in our school, I have the amazing opportunity to expose children to things for the first time. I take that responsibility very seriously, and I consider it a great privilege and work very hard to make sure that we are learning about a variety of traditions, religions, cultures, and so on.

VERA: What have you noticed in your students/children as a result of rebellious read alouds?

DANYA: Children are hungry for new vocabulary and new lenses through which to see the world. As we read new books, learn about new foods, celebrations, customs, it quickly becomes integrated into their play and their drawings. Young children are also sticklers for equity and fairness, so once they learn about transgender people, or discrimination in general, they are hyper aware of it and will bring it to their teachers when they see it in their lives.

VERA: What is one tip or piece of advice you would give to educators?

DANYA: Always preread. This goes for every book you are going to read to the class but especially a book that might have vocabulary that you are not familiar with. If there is a word you do not know, find out how to pronounce it; when you read it out loud, if you're not sure, you can play it on your phone, model for your students "this is a word that is unfamiliar to me but I want to get it right because I want to show respect to this character to learn how to say their name (or holiday)."

If you are hoping to convey a particular concept to young students, I find that choosing two or three books that deal with the same concept works very well to help students form connections and generate questions.

VERA: What are your top five favorite read alouds?

DANYA: This is too hard to limit to five but I'll try!

- *Green Pants* by Kenneth Kraegel
- *Neither* by Airlie Anderson
- *Where the Wild Things Are* by Maurice Sendak
- *The Rabbit Listened* by Corri Doerrfield
- *Stuck* by Oliver Jeffers

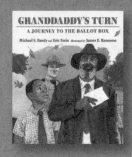

LEARNING FOR JUSTICE STANDARDS

Identity
Diversity
Justice

ELA STANDARDS

- Students will ask and answer questions about key details in a text.

- Students will acknowledge differences in the points of view of characters.

- Students will describe how characters in a story respond to major events and challenges.

This unit is full of nonfiction books. I wanted to be sure to include a few nonfiction titles that would invite conversations around history. Sometimes, as educators we shy away from conversations around history because we're unsure what is the "right" thing to say or how we can provide a nonbiased perspective. Using nonfiction books, we can invite students to think of the ways in which history may be repeating itself and how different events in history have affected their own lives.

GRANDDADDY'S TURN: A JOURNEY TO THE BALLOT BOX

Written by Michael S. Bandy and Eric Stein
Illustrated by James E. Ransome

BOOK BIOGRAPHY

Michael enjoys spending time with his grandfather. He learns so much from him. One day, Michael and his grandfather take a trip that will change both of their lives forever.

VERA'S VIEW

My Papa (grandfather) would tell me stories of racism he faced as a Black man in the United States. As I listened to these stories, I imagined how my Papa, this strong-willed, intelligent, powerhouse of a man, could ever have endured experiences of hatred, racism, and unnecessary unkindness. As an adult, I realize he endured for me. For me to receive my education at a private institution, for me to excel in my career, for me to be able to share his story (and the story of many Black Americans) with you today.

When I read *Granddaddy's Turn*, I often think of my Papa. I think of all the Black Americans who were denied their basic rights.

START SMALL

Opening pages (double spread)

What do you notice? Who are the members of this family?

BE CONSISTENT

We worked together a lot … (page)

Patience means to wait for something in a calm manner. Sometimes it can be difficult to be patient. What are some things you have had to be patient for? How do you practice being patient when you really want something to happen?

Where are all the rides and animals? (page)

What do you notice about the flags on this page? Do you know what both of those flags symbolize? How does the Confederate flag help you understand what might happen to the granddad? What do you notice about the people waiting in line to vote?

Anybody in my family had ever … (pages)

How has Michael shown patience in this story? How has the granddad shown patience throughout his life? Is it fair to have to be patient for something that everyone else has? Is it fair to have to be patient for something you are being denied because of your race?

> Rebel reader, I want you to remember that the experience you will read in this story still happens to this very day. If you want more information on what you can do to stop voter suppression, please visit these websites:
>
> ACLU: https://www.aclu.org/issues/voting-rights/fighting-voter-suppression
>
> Voting Rights Alliance: https://www.votingrightsalliance.org/forms-of-voter-suppression

KEEP CONSTANT

Voter suppression is a form of systematic racism. Systemic racism is a type of racism that shows up in the laws of a country or the rules of an organization. Voter suppression is used to keep people of color from exercising their right to vote. Today voter suppression looks like long lines in the cold or heat, police at polling places, strict photo ID laws, not offering early voting, or lack of language options.

LET'S MAKE A PLAN OF ACTION

- What is the history of voter suppression in the area you live in?
- How can you help to end voter suppression in your community?
- What are other forms of systemic racism?

Because I read this book, I now know _____ .

Because I read this book, I wonder _____ .

Because I read this book, I understand _____ .

LEARNING FOR JUSTICE STANDARDS

Identity
Diversity
Justice
Action

ELA STANDARDS

- Students will ask and answer questions about key details in a text.

- Students will acknowledge differences in the points of view of characters.

- Students will describe how characters in a story respond to major events and challenges.

MAGIC RAMEN: THE STORY OF MOMOFUKU ANDO

Written by Andrea Wang
Illustrated by Kana Urbanowicz

BOOK BIOGRAPHY

Momofuku Ando watched the people in his country live in despair after World War II. He wanted to find a way to give people nourishment and hope. He worked tirelessly on a recipe that would benefit the most needy.

VERA'S VIEW

I struggled with whether to place this book in the food, actions, or history section. I ultimately decided it should go under history because what Momofuku did changed the history of Japan *and* food forever. I love this story about persistence, perseverance, inspiration, and, more importantly, a delicious meal!

START SMALL

Opening pages (double spread)

What do you notice? What does the word *ruins* mean?

BE CONSISTENT

Bad harvests, rationing, and war… (pages)

Sometimes we think the only effects of war are people who died or were injured. More often, there are longer lasting effects. The people in Osaka faced food scarcity after World War II. How do you think people who had no money survived?

Ando kept experimenting with different… (pages)

Ando continued to struggle to find a recipe that worked even though he continued to fail. Why do you think Ando never gave up? Why was his perseverance especially important at this point in history?

After a year of trying… (pages)

Ando invented instant ramen! Do you think that much of Japan was still recovering from the war after one year? Do you think Ando's instant ramen was still necessary? Why or why not?

KEEP CONSTANT

Momofuku Ando found inspiration during despair. His tireless work helped save many people in his country from dying of hunger. His company, Nissin Foods, continues to donate packages of ramen to those experiencing homelessness or displacement after a national disaster.

LET'S MAKE A PLAN OF ACTION

- Who are other people who found ways to help others during a time of tragedy or despair?
- What are some ways we can help areas that have suffered from war or violence?
- How can we use our own skills, services, or talents to help others?

Because I read this book, I now know _____ .

Because I read this book, I wonder _____ .

Because I read this book, I understand _____ .

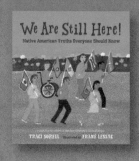

WE ARE STILL HERE

Written by Traci Sorell
Illustrated by Frane Lessac

BOOK BIOGRAPHY

We Are Still Here showcases the challenges Native Nations have faced in the United States. We witness students presenting on various points in U.S. history. This is an important and in-depth perspective on the Native American experience.

VERA'S VIEW

I learned more about Native American history in this picture book than I have in my entire educational career. This book is chock full of information. It's so important to share this book with students so that they may develop an accurate and thorough understanding of Native Nations.

START SMALL

Opening pages (double spread)

Whose land are you currently living on? You can visit https://native-land.ca/ to learn more.

BE CONSISTENT

Indian New Deal...(pages 10-11)

What do you think about the Indian New Deal? Was it fair? Look at the illustration. What do you notice about the people signing the deal?

Relocation...(pages 14-15)

What do you notice about the location of the people on this page? Was relocation fair? How do you think this affected communities of Native people?

Religious Freedom...(pages 22-23)

What do you notice about the supreme court judges? Are or were any of the judges Native? Native Nations were not allowed to practice their religions or speak their languages. How do you think that affected Native people?

KEEP CONSTANT

The words "We Are Still Here!" continue to repeat throughout the story. Unfortunately, many textbooks and educators continue to portray Native Americans/ Indigenous people in the past tense. Native Americans are very much still here, and it's imperative to continue to integrate Native American history, accomplishments, people, and contributions into our curriculum throughout the school year.

LET'S MAKE A PLAN OF ACTION

- What is the Native American/Indigenous history of the place where you live today?
- What are the ways we can support Native American/Indigenous tribes in the areas where we live?
- How are the stories of Native American/Indigenous people taught in your school? What books and images are used, and do those books or images tell an accurate and current story of Native/Indigenous peoples?

Because I read this book, I now know _____.

Because I read this book, I wonder _____.

Because I read this book, I understand _____.

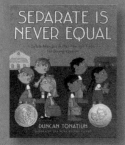

LEARNING FOR JUSTICE STANDARDS

Identity
Diversity
Justice
Action

ELA STANDARDS

- Students will ask and answer questions about key details in a text.

- Students will acknowledge differences in the points of view of characters.

- Students will describe how characters in a story respond to major events and challenges.

SEPARATE IS NEVER EQUAL

Written and illustrated by Duncan Tonatiuh

BOOK BIOGRAPHY

Sylvia Mendez's family lived and worked in Westminster, California. When their aunt went to enroll the children in the nearest school, the Mendez children were denied enrollment into the all-white school in Westminster. Instead, they were told to attend the Mexican school farther away. *Separate Is Never Equal* is the true story of how the Mendez family fought to end segregation in schools in California.

VERA'S VIEW

While I am very familiar with the *Brown v. Board of Education* case, which ended segregation across the United States, I had very little knowledge of the Mendez family's efforts, which happened seven years before *Brown v. Board of Ed.* The injustices of segregation are long and far reaching. This story is powerful and provides an additional perspective on the racial injustices that are a part of U.S. history.

START SMALL

Opening pages (double spread)

What do you notice? What would you do or say if you heard someone say what the young white boy said?

BE CONSISTENT

When they arrived home... (pages 12-13)

What do you think Sylvia's father is thinking? What do you think the superintendent is thinking? The superintendent doesn't give Sylvia's father a reason for why his children can't attend the Westminster school. What do you think his reason might be?

Over the next few months... (pages 20-21)

What do you notice about Sylvia's mother? Often women aren't featured in the forefront of civil rights movements, when they in fact have played an important role in organizing, community building, and ensuring family structures stay in place.

KEEP CONSTANT

The work to desegregate places was difficult after the Supreme Court ruled that separate was equal (*Plessy v. Ferguson*). In 1896, the Supreme Court ruled that places could racially segregate spaces as long as those spaces were "equal" in quality. After reading this story we learned that these separate spaces were never truly equal in quality, specifically for Black and Brown people.

LET'S MAKE A PLAN OF ACTION

- What is the segregation history of the place where you live today?
- Where do we see racial segregation happening now?
- What can you do if you notice racial segregation happening in the spaces you're in?

Because I read this book, I now know _____.

Because I read this book, I wonder _____.

Because I read this book, I understand _____.

LEARNING FOR JUSTICE STANDARDS

Identity
Diversity
Justice
Action

ELA STANDARDS

- Students will ask and answer questions about key details in a text.
- Students will acknowledge differences in the points of view of characters.
- Students will describe how characters in a story respond to major events and challenges.
- Students will compare and contrast the adventures and experiences of characters in stories.

THE OLDEST STUDENT

Written by Rita Lorraine Hubbard
Illustrated by Oge Mora

BOOK BIOGRAPHY

Mary Walker was born into enslavement. Being enslaved meant she did not have access to an education. Instead, she and her family were forced to work long, arduous hours on a plantation. It wasn't until Mary was fifteen that she was able to live her life in her own way. She went on to get married and have children, but there was one thing she hadn't accomplished: the ability to read. This is the story of how Mary Walker learned to read at 116 years old.

VERA'S VIEW

I absolutely love this story. It showcases how Black people continue to thrive despite the barriers set up against us. Mary Walker learning to read at 116 is also an important lesson to the students in our classrooms. Learning something new is hard and can take time. It's OK if something doesn't stick right away, but don't give up on something you want to do.

START SMALL

She knew the second rule… (page 3)

Why do you think enslaved people weren't taught how to read or write? How do you think this affected enslaved people's lives?

BE CONSISTENT

When she was fifteen... (double spread)

Do you think Mary (and other previously enslaved people) has an easier life now? Why or why not? What are some burdens or obstacles she may face? How might the inability to read and write affect her life now that she is freed?

For the next year... (pages)

Have you ever tried to learn something new? Was it easy or hard for you? Can you imagine what it must have been like for Mary to learn to read at 116? Think of all the experiences she had in her life and how hard she had to work to be able to provide for herself and her family while not knowing how to read or write.

What obstacles, other than age, might Mary be up against?

KEEP CONSTANT

When discussing America's history of enslavement, it is important to use the correct words to describe what was happening during this time. Between approximately 1619 until 1865, it was legal in America to enslave people. We use the term *enslaved person* instead of *slave* to give humanity to the person who was forced to work for someone. We should focus the negative on the person who is doing something terrible, not on the person who is subjected to atrocity.

LET'S MAKE A PLAN OF ACTION

- How can you help practice "person first" language when you are talking about the experiences of other people?
- How can you practice supporting someone who is learning something new and is finding it difficult?
- How can we use our understanding of the treatment of enslaved people to make efforts to take action when we see racism today?

Because I read this book, I now know _____ .

Because I read this book, I wonder _____ .

Because I read this book, I understand _____ .

TEACHER TALK

FEATURED EDUCATOR: Laura Page

Montgomery, Texas. Ninth through twelfth grades. Parent of one child, age 8. White, cisgender. Pronouns: she/her.

VERA: Can you talk to me a bit about your experience with reading or teaching "controversial" topics through read alouds?

LAURA: I think that using read alouds is a really great way to introduce controversial topics because it already introduces a new perspective and new characters, which kids already love.

VERA: What are some challenges you've faced?

LAURA: At my school and in my district, it is expected that we do not discuss any "controversial" topics or have any political discussions of any kind. I completely disagree with this, and so that is why it is important for me to have these important conversations about race, class, sexuality, and so on with my child at home.

VERA: Why is the work of integrating "controversial" books into your child's life important or meaningful to you?

LAURA: I want my child to be aware that she comes from privilege, and I want her to do more than just acknowledge that. I want her to be exposed to as much as possible, as young as possible, so that she knows how to interact with all types of people.

VERA: What have you noticed from your child as a result of rebellious read alouds?

LAURA: My daughter is really so much more aware of her surroundings, toys, and other media that she consumes. If we are watching a TV show that is all white characters, she notices. She wanted to get Pride merchandise during the summer because her aunts are lesbians and she wanted to show that she supports them. We were playing Barbies, and she noticed we only had a couple of Black Barbies and she wanted to buy more. She noticed all the Barbies are thin and wanted to buy the larger sized Barbies. I just think she's thinking more about the world around her.

VERA: What is one tip or piece of advice you would give to parents/caregivers?

LAURA: I think just to start introducing your child to as much as possible. There are age-appropriate ways to have every conversation. Kids notice everything, so not talking about something just makes kids think certain things are bad or shouldn't be talked about.

PART THREE

communicating with Parents, Administrators, and Colleagues

I assume you picked up this book because you're teaching in a school environment that encourages culturally responsive teaching and open conversations that lead to critical thinking. However, the very nature of rebelliousness means that you may teach in a school that hasn't quite embraced this work. Either way, in the United States today, inviting conversations about race, gender, traditions, or anything considered outside traditional curriculum can be fraught. I encourage you to find colleagues, whether in your building, in your district, or online, who you can talk with and bounce ideas around with. You can even try some practice read alouds together to plan and anticipate how conversations might go so you don't feel so vulnerable in the moment. I encourage you to reach out to me, too, and to engage with the community that has built up around my Instagram accounts, @thetututeacher and @diversereads.

WHAT ABOUT PARENTS/CAREGIVERS?

Hands down, whenever I speak with educators about the importance of creating an inclusive library, I am asked, "But what about the parents/caregivers?"

To that I say, "What about them?"

And I know that answer comes with a bit of privilege and sounds like a nonchalant attitude; you may not teach in the same type of environment that I do. But here's what I know: it is our job as educators to ensure that each child in our class feels respected, cared for, and seen. How can we do this when we neglect to include books or refuse to invite conversations just because doing so might upset a parent or caregiver?

When I'm asked, "But what about the parents/caregivers?" I think, "What about the kids?"

- What about the child who has two mothers and never sees their family celebrated during the read alouds in a family unit?

- What about the student who celebrates Yom Kippur and sees only decor that celebrates Christian holidays plastered around the hallways of their school?

- What about the Black student who sees only stories that feature white or animal characters?

- What about the child who has a disability and deals with countless questions from peers?

- What about the child whose name is never pronounced correctly?

- What about the student who is mocked during lunch time for having food that is different from what other students are eating?

- What about the student who is teased for having an eye shape that is different from other students?

- What about the student who sits in class after class never learning about their Indigenous history in school?

- What about the student who is never given the opportunity to learn that their voice matters, that their experience is important, and that even children as young as them can make a difference?

Another thing I know: parents and caregivers can be important partners. And I know that one way to ensure that our classroom conversations ripple outward is to involve parents in the learning right from the start. Here are some ideas to answer that big question: What about parents?

CLASSROOM NEWSLETTER

One way that I share our learning with those at home is to include the covers of the books we are reading in our monthly newsletter. This invites families to continue some of these conversations at home or ask questions about their learning around a particular book. These are examples of recent newsletters from my classroom.

CURRICULUM NIGHT

Additionally, at our Back to School night, I remind parents and caregivers that their student is part of an inclusive classroom. We are a classroom that embraces everyone and invites curiosity and questioning. Setting the tone around expectations at the beginning of the year helps parents and caregivers understand that their student is in a space that will be accepting of everyone.

Looking to talk to parents and caregivers about the importance of including these books? Check out the International Literacy Association's Children's Rights to Read:

1. Children have the basic human right to read.

2. Children have the right to access texts in print and digital formats.

3. Children have the right to choose what they read.

4. Children have the right to read texts that mirror their experiences and languages, provide windows into the lives of others, and open doors into our diverse world.

5. Children have the right to read for pleasure.

6. Children have the right to supportive reading environments with knowledgeable literacy partners.

7. Children have the right to extended time set aside for reading.

8. Children have the right to share what they learn through reading by collaborating with others locally and globally.

9. Children have the right to read as a springboard for other forms of communication, such as writing, speaking, and visually representing.

10. Children have the right to benefit from the financial and material resources of governments, agencies, and organizations that support reading and reading instruction.

Reprinted with permission from the International Literacy Association.

You can download a poster of these rights from the International Literacy Association website: https://bit.ly/3Bz3Yp2.

COMMUNITY AND FAMILY EVENTS

My current school has something called Family Friday. Parents and caregivers are encouraged to come to the classrooms and do an activity or read a book with the class. I love these days! It creates a wonderful opportunity for caregivers to share their culture, language, traditions, and more with students. It affirms that caregivers are an integral part of the whole child's learning experience. If your school encourages these opportunities, it can be a wonderful chance to invite parents and caregivers to join the rebellion.

DO-TOGETHER ACTIVITIES

If a special event is not practical or possible in your school, try something simpler. Try sending home activities periodically that include families in sharing what makes them and their child's experiences and background special. These can be shared in class or on a special bulletin board. The snowflake homework below is a seasonal hit year after year for the students and families in my classroom.

Snowflake Homework

It's finally winter! The winter season also brings a new year and a time to reflect. Your student is bringing home a snowflake to add to our Kindergarten wall. Please help your student decorate the snowflake. Make a snowflake that is as unique as you are! The snowflake can be decorated with pictures or words that describe how unique and special you are.
Be creative!
We want this project to be fun and meaningful to you. Please be sure to cut out the snowflake before returning it to school.
Thanks for your help with this project.
The snowflake is due January 31st.
Thank you!
Kindergarten Team

WHAT ABOUT ADMIN?

It's true, the issue of unsupportive administration can be tricky. How do you continue to do what you know is right when your administration is telling you not to? In these situations, I would encourage educators to consider a few things:

- Did your administration make you aware this was their viewpoint *before* you were hired?
- Do you feel comfortable and safe in a school environment that does not embrace inclusion?
- How much influence does your administration have on the curriculum you teach?

Ultimately, if an educator is at a school that will not support their role in the rebellion, then it may be time to consider another place of employment. And I completely understand that this isn't always the easiest (or most cost-effective) decision. So the following are some suggestions for ensuring administration buy-in, just in case you receive pushback on your instructional decisions.

CLASSROOM LIBRARY TOUR

Offer a tour of your classroom library before the first day of school. Show your enthusiasm for the books, and share a couple of the lessons in this book so that your principal can see the learning standards that will be met.

Additionally, take an inventory of your classroom (or school) library. Use the results to show the lack of inclusive literature in the library and as a rallying cry for the start of a necessary rebellion.

CLARIFY LEARNING INTENTIONS

Make sure your administrator knows that these are conversations where all viewpoints are welcome, questions are surfaced, and more research and learning are encouraged. Remind them that your role is simply facilitating conversations, not imparting ideology or indoctrination. (These are the big scary words used to thwart discussion and critical thinking!)

This is also a great time to reference the learning standards you're keeping in mind during your read alouds. Use your students' journal entries or anecdotal evidence to show that not only does this work build skills needed to meet learning standards, but it's also important to developing citizens!

OFFER AN INVITATION!

Invite your administrator to participate in a read aloud with you and your students. The kids will feel so special, and the administrator will have a firsthand look into the conversation to see that what's mentioned above is true. Additionally, show your administrator the powerful and thoughtful connections your students are making *because* of the work they're doing with these read alouds.

WHAT ABOUT COLLEAGUES?

Marching down the road of rebellion alone can seem overwhelming and at times impossible. Finding a colleague to join you as you promote inclusion and diversity can make the learning and growth for both students and teachers incredibly powerful. But what do you do when you work with colleagues who don't encourage the rebellion? Here are just a few suggestions to help:

- Similar to your work with admin, invite your colleagues into your classroom during a read aloud. Let them hear and see the powerful work your students are doing.

- Gift them your favorite rebellious read aloud. I know, this seems silly—why would you gift someone something that they are so against? But sometimes people just need a gentle push. They might not know where or how to start. By simply giving them a rebellious read-aloud title, you may have just given them a key to unlocking unknown potential.

- Ask curious questions. Here are some examples:

  o What are some of your favorite read alouds? How do you feel when you share those stories with your students? Can I talk to you about some of the experiences I've had reading diverse texts to my students?

  o Can you talk to me a little bit about why you don't want to read these titles to your students?

  o I was nervous about that (e.g., the parent/caregiver response), too. Can I talk to you about how I overcame that feeling?

Everyone enters the path to rebellion on their own time. Whether they enter with you, before you, or after you (days, months, or even years later), it's key to remember that this important, thoughtful, and meaningful work is not only for ourselves, but more importantly for our students.

EPILOGUE: WISHES

What do I wish for this book?

I wish this book encourages you to invite students into a new way of learning about the world around them.

I wish that each of you reading this book feels a bit of validation—the validation that comes with knowing this work is the right work.

I wish for you to continue. This is only the beginning. There is so much work to be done. Work that may have started with a read aloud but grows into your own rebellion.

I wish that one day these conversations aren't known as "rebellious" and are just typical conversations teachers have with their students.

I wish that we adults will have more conversations with one another about "hushed" topics so that fear and misunderstanding can evolve into advocacy and allyship.

I wish for the students in our care to grow up knowing that conversations are acceptable, that asking questions is OK, that listening to others tell their stories is necessary.

I wish that each student walks through our classroom doors feeling validated, respected, seen, and heard.

I wish that with my whole heart.

Appendix

ADDITIONAL CHILDREN'S BOOK SELECTIONS

If I had all the time and money in the world, I would sit and create lists of wonderful books for you to use in your classrooms. I struggled limiting the lessons in this book only to forty-five. I wanted to go on and on and on. However, I hope you're left with enough to get the conversations flowing. In case you're looking for a few more texts to help you continue the conversations, here are twenty-five titles that just give me that "Ahhh! I love this book so much" feeling inside. These are listed alphabetically by author's last name, not in any order of topic.

You Have a Voice
Written by Vera Ahiyya (That's me! I wrote a children's book, y'all.)
Illustrated by Fabiana Faiall

Isabel and Her Colores Go to School
Written by Alexandra Alessandri
Illustrated by Courtney Dawson

Soul Food Sunday
Written by Wingsome Bingham
Illustrated by Charles G. Esperanza

The Cot in the Living Room
Written by Hilda Eunice Burgos
Illustrated by Gaby D'Alessandro

What Happened to You?
Written by James Catchpole
Illustrated by Karen George

We Move Together
Written by Kelly Fritsch and Anne McGuire
Illustrated by Eduardo Trejos

Change Sings: A Children's Anthem
Written by Amanda Gorman
Illustrated by Loren Long

A Day for Rememberin'
Written by Leah Henderson
Illustrated by Floyd Cooper

Eyes That Speak to the Stars
Written by Joanna Ho
Illustrated by Dung Ho

Home for a While
Written by Lauren Kerstein
Illustrated by Natalia Moore

The Arabic Quilt: An Immigrant Story
Written by Aya Khalil
Illustrated by Anait Semirdzhyan

Black Cowboy, Wild Horses
Written by Julius Lester
Illustrated by Jerry Pinkney

What Are Your Words?
Written by Katherine Locke
Illustrated by Anne/Andy Passchier

Ohana Means Family
Written by Ilima Loomis
Illustrated by Kenard Pak

Being You: A First Conversation About Gender
Written by Megan Madison and Jessica Ralli
Illustrated by Anne/Andy Passchier

Not Little
Written by Maya Myers
Illustrated by Hyewon Yu

If Dominican Were a Color
Written by Sili Recio
Illustrated by Brianna McCarthy

Fauja Singh Keeps Going
Written by Simran Jeet Singh
Illustrated by Baljinder Kaur

Dumpling Day
Written by Meera Sriram
Illustrated by Ins De Antuano

Classified: The Secret Career of Mary Golda Ross
Written by Traci Sorell
Illustrated by Natasha Donovan

Powwow Day
Written by Traci Sorell
Illustrated by Madelyn Goodnight

When Lola Visits
Written by Michelle Sterling
Illustrated by Aaron Asis

Little Things: A Story About Acts of Kindness
Written by Christian Trimmer
Illustrated by Kaylani Juanita

The Rice in the Pot Goes Round and Round
Written by Wendy Wan-Long Shang
Illustrated by Lorian Tu

Watercress
Written by Andrea Wang
Illustrated by Jason Chin

SAMPLE TIMELINE

I know that planning out your year (or month/week/day) is essential in ensuring lessons actually get taught. So I thought it would be helpful if I included a timeline of how the lessons in this book fall throughout the school year. This is a suggestion, of course, but this timeline is helpful if you think about the progression of conversations and the learning development of your students.

- August/September—Our Names Are Important
- October—Our Features Are Important
- November—Our Disabilities Are Important
- December—Our Families Are Important
- January—Our Foods Are Important
- February—Our Traditions Are Important
- March—Our Identities Are Important
- April—Our Histories Are Important
- May/June—Our Actions Are Important

Classroom Library Student Interview

- Scan the QR code or access online at resources.corwin.com/rebellious.

Scan the QR code to access the companion website. resources.corwin .com/rebellious

RECOMMENDED RESOURCES

WEBSITES

Facing History and Ourselves: https://www.facinghistory.org/

Learning For Justice: https://www.learningforjustice.org/

Rethinking Schools: https://rethinkingschools.org/

SOCIAL MEDIA

Instagram

@teachandtransform

@teachingoutsidethebinary

@spencer2thewest

@blm_edu_ny

@crutches_and_spice

@tiplerteaches

@readlikearockstarteaching

@apron_education

ADDITIONAL TITLES BY TOPIC

OUR NAMES ARE IMPORTANT

- *My Name Is Sangeol* by Karen Lynn Williams and Khadra Mohammed
- *Name Jar* by Yangsook Choi
- *Alma and How She Got Her Name* by Juana Martinez-Neal
- *My Name Is Maria Isabel* by Alma Flor Ada
- *Thao: A Picture Book* by Thao Lam

OUR FEATURES ARE IMPORTANT

- *Bodies Are Cool* by Tyler Feder
- *Our Skin* by Megan Madison and Jessica Ralli
- *Eyes That Speak to the Stars* by Joanna Ho
- *The Proudest Color* by Sheila Modir and Jeffrey Kashou
- *Beautifully Me* by Nabela Noor

OUR TRADITIONS ARE IMPORTANT

- *Playing With Lanterns* by Wang Yage
- *Pumpkin Pie for Sigd: A Holiday Tale* by Jennifer Tzivia MacLeod
- *Powwow Day* by Traci Sorell
- *The Shadow in the Moon* by Christian Matula
- *Lighting Our World* by Catherine Rondina

OUR ACTIONS ARE IMPORTANT

- *Alejandria Fights Back!/¡La Lucha de Alejandria!* by Leticia Hernández-Linares
- *Kamala and Maya's Big Idea* by Meena Harris
- *Change Sings: A Children's Anthem* by Amanda Gorman
- *Little Things: A Story About Acts of Kindness* by Christian Trimmer
- *I Can Help* by Reem Faruqi

OUR FAMILIES ARE IMPORTANT

- *Where Three Oceans Meet* by Rajani LaRocca
- *Grandpa Across the Ocean* by Hyewon Yum
- *The Cot in the Living Room* by Hilda Eunice Burgos

- *Mango Moon: When Deportation Divides a Family* by Diane de Anda
- *Drawn Together* by Minh Lê

OUR IDENTITIES ARE IMPORTANT

- *Calvin* by JR Ford and Vanessa Ford
- *The Proudest Blue: A Story of Hijab and Family* by Ibtihaj Muhammad
- *Areli Is a Dreamer: A True Story* by Areli Morales
- *A DACA Recipient* by Areli Morales
- *Being You: A First Conversation About Gender* by Megan Madison and Jessica Ralli
- *It Feels Good to Be Yourself: A Book About Gender Identity* by Theresa Thorn

OUR DISABILITIES ARE IMPORTANT

- *Different—A Great Thing to Be!* by Heather Avis
- *What Happened to You?* by James Catchpole
- *All the Way to the Top: How One Girl's Fight for Americans With Disabilities Changed Everything* by Annette Bay Pimentel
- *Meeting Mimi: A Story About Different Abilities* by Francie Dolan
- *We Move Together* by Kelly Fritsch and Anne McGuire

OUR FOODS ARE IMPORTANT

- *Kalamata's Kitchen* by Sarah Thomas
- *Soul Food Sunday* by Winsome Bingham
- *Saturday at the Food Pantry* by Diane O'Neill
- *Dumpling Day* by Meera Sriram
- *Chaiwala!* by Priti Birla Maheshwari
- *May Your Life Be Deliciosa* by Michael Genhart

OUR HISTORIES ARE IMPORTANT

- *Child of the Flower-Song People: Luz Jiménez, Daughter of the Nahua* by Gloria Amescua
- *¡Mambo Mucho Mambo! The Dance That Crossed Color Lines* by Dean Robbins
- *Sharice's Big Voice: A Native Kid Becomes a Congresswoman* by Sharice Davids
- *June Almeida, Virus Detective! The Woman Who Discovered the First Human Coronavirus* by Suzanne Slade
- *The 1619 Project: Born on the Water* by Nikole Hannah-Jones

REBELLIOUS READ ALOUDS AT A GLANCE: LIST OF BOOKS AND LEARNING STANDARDS

Book Title	Learning for Justice Standards	Literacy Standards
A Different Pond Written by Bao Phi Illustrated by Thi Bui	Identity Diversity Justice	• Students will ask and answer questions about key details in a text. • Students will acknowledge differences in the points of view of characters. • Students will describe how characters in a story respond to major events and challenges.
Alma and How She Got Her Name Written and illustrated by Juana Martinez-Neal	Identity Diversity	• Students will acknowledge differences in the points of view of characters. • Students will describe how characters in a story respond to major events and challenges.
Alejandria Fights Back!/¡La Lucha de Alejandria! Written by/ Escrito por Leticia Hernández-Linares and the Rise-Home Stories Project Illustrated by/ ilustrado por Robert Liu-Trujillo Translated by/ traducido por Carla España	Identity Diversity Justice Action	• Students will ask and answer questions about key details in a text. • Students will acknowledge differences in the points of view of characters. • Students will describe how characters in a story respond to major events and challenges.
Always Anjali Written by Sheetal Sheth Illustrated by Jessica Blank	Identity Diversity Justice Action	• Students will ask and answer questions about key details in a text. • Students will acknowledge differences in the points of view of characters. • Students will describe how characters in a story respond to major events and challenges.
All Because You Matter Written by Tami Charles Illustrated by Bryan Collier	Identity Diversity Justice Action	• Students will ask and answer questions about key details in a text. • Students will acknowledge differences in the points of view of characters. • Students will describe how characters in a story respond to major events and challenges.

(Continued)

(Continued)

Book Title	Learning for Justice Standards	Literacy Standards
All the Way to the Top: How One Girl's Fight for Americans With Disabilities Changed Everything Written by Annette Bay Pimentel Illustrated by Nabi H. Ali	Identity Diversity Justice Action	• Students will ask and answer questions about key details in a text. • Students will acknowledge differences in the points of view of characters. • Students will describe how characters in a story respond to major events and challenges. • Students will compare and contrast the adventures and experiences of characters in stories.
Amira's Picture Day Written by Reem Faruqi Illustrated by Fahmida Azim	Identity Diversity	• Students will ask and answer questions about key details in a text. • Students will acknowledge differences in the points of view of characters. • Students will compare and contrast the adventures and experiences of characters in stories.
Areli Is a Dreamer: A True Story Written by Areli Morales Illustrated by Luisa Uribe	Identity Diversity	• Students will ask and answer questions about key details in a text. • Students will acknowledge differences in the points of view of characters. • Students will describe how characters in a story respond to major events and challenges.
Awesomely Emma: A Charley and Emma Story Written by Amy Webb Illustrated by Merrilee Liddiard	Identity Diversity Justice Action	• Students will ask and answer questions about key details in a text. • Students will acknowledge differences in the points of view of characters. • Students will compare and contrast the adventures and experiences of characters in stories. • Students will describe how characters in a story respond to major events and challenges.
Beautifully Me Written by Nabela Noor Illustrated by Nabi H. Ali	Identity Diversity	• Students will ask and answer questions about key details in a text. • Students will acknowledge differences in the points of view of characters. • Students will compare and contrast the adventures and experiences of characters in stories.

Book Title	Learning for Justice Standards	Literacy Standards
Becoming Vanessa Written and illustrated by Vanessa Brantley-Newton	Identity Diversity Justice Action	• Students will ask and answer questions about key details in a text. • Students will acknowledge differences in the points of view of characters. • Students will describe how characters in a story respond to major events and challenges.
Bilal Cooks Daal Written by Aisha Saeed Illustrated by Anoosha Syed	Identity Diversity	• Students will ask and answer questions about key details in a text. • Students will acknowledge differences in the points of view of characters. • Students will describe how characters in a story respond to major events and challenges. • Students will compare and contrast the adventures and experiences of characters in stories.
Black Is a Rainbow Color Written by Angela Joy Illustrated by Ekua Holmes	Identity Diversity	• Students will ask and answer questions about key details in a text. • Students will acknowledge differences in the points of view of characters. • Students will compare and contrast the adventures and experiences of characters in stories.
Call Me Max Written by Kyle Lukoff Illustrated by Luciano Lozano	Identity Diversity Justice Action	• Students will ask and answer questions about key details in a text. • Students will acknowledge differences in the points of view of characters. • Students will describe how characters in a story respond to major events and challenges.
Chicken Soup, Chicken Soup Written by Pamela Mayer Illustrated by Deborah Melmon	Identity Diversity	• Students will ask and answer questions about key details in a text. • Students will acknowledge differences in the points of view of characters. • Students will describe how characters in a story respond to major events and challenges. • Students will compare and contrast the adventures and experiences of characters in stories.

(Continued)

(Continued)

Book Title	Learning for Justice Standards	Literacy Standards
Evelyn Del Rey Is Moving Away Written by Meg Medina Illustrated by Sonia Sánchez	Identity Diversity Action	• Students will ask and answer questions about key details in a text. • Students will acknowledge differences in the points of view of characters. • Students will compare and contrast the adventures and experiences of characters in stories. • Students will describe how characters in a story respond to major events and challenges.
Eyes That Kiss in the Corners Written by Joanna Ho Illustrated by Dung Ho	Identity Diversity	• Students will ask and answer questions about key details in a text. • Students will acknowledge differences in the points of view of characters. • Students will identify words and phrases in stories or poems that suggest feelings or appeal to the senses.
Freedom Soup Written by Tami Charles Illustrated by Jacqueline Alcántara	Identity Diversity	• Students will ask and answer questions about key details in a text. • Students will acknowledge differences in the points of view of characters. • Students will compare and contrast the adventures and experiences of characters in stories. • Students will describe how characters in a story respond to major events and challenges.
Fry Bread: A Native American Family Story Written by Kevin Noble Maillard Illustrated by Juana Martinez-Neal	Identity Diversity	• Students will ask and answer questions about key details in a text. • Students will acknowledge differences in the points of view of characters.
Granddaddy's Turn: A Journey to the Ballot Box Written by Michael S. Bandy and Eric Stein Illustrated by James E. Ransome	Identity Diversity Justice	• Students will ask and answer questions about key details in a text. • Students will acknowledge differences in the points of view of characters. • Students will describe how characters in a story respond to major events and challenges.

Book Title	Learning for Justice Standards	Literacy Standards
Grandpa Grumps Written by Katrina Moore Illustrated by Xindi Yan	Identity Diversity	• Students will ask and answer questions about key details in a text. • Students will acknowledge differences in the points of view of characters. • Students will describe how characters in a story respond to major events and challenges. • Students will compare and contrast the adventures and experiences of characters in stories.
Hair Twins Written by Raakhee Mirchandani Illustrated by Holly Hatam	Identity Diversity	• Students will ask and answer questions about key details in a text. • Students will acknowledge differences in the points of view of characters. • Students will compare and contrast the adventures and experiences of characters in stories.
I Talk Like a River Written by Jordan Scott Illustrated by Sydney Smith	Identity Diversity Justice Action	• Students will ask and answer questions about key details in a text. • Students will acknowledge differences in the points of view of characters. • Students will compare and contrast the adventures and experiences of characters in stories. • Students will describe how characters in a story respond to major events and challenges.
IntersectionAllies: We Make Room for All Written by Chelsea Johnson, LaToya Council, and Carolyn Choi Illustrated by Ashley Seil Smith	Identity Diversity Justice Action	• Students will ask and answer questions about key details in a text. • Students will acknowledge differences in the points of view of characters. • Students will describe how characters in a story respond to major events and challenges. • Students will compare and contrast the adventures and experiences of characters in stories.
Laxmi's Mooch Written by Shelly Anand Illustrated by Nabi H. Ali	Identity Diversity	• Students will ask and answer questions about key details in a text. • Students will acknowledge differences in the points of view of characters. • Students will identify words and phrases in stories or poems that suggest feelings or appeal to the senses.

(Continued)

(Continued)

Book Title	Learning for Justice Standards	Literacy Standards
Magic Ramen: The Story of Momofuku Ando Written by Andrea Wang Illustrated by Kana Urbanowicz	Diversity Justice Action	• Students will ask and answer questions about key details in a text. • Students will acknowledge differences in the points of view of characters. • Students will describe how characters in a story respond to major events and challenges.
Malala's Magic Pencil Written by Malala Yousafzai Illustrated by Kerasoët	Identity Diversity Justice Action	• Students will ask and answer questions about key details in a text. • Students will acknowledge differences in the points of view of characters. • Students will describe how characters in a story respond to major events and challenges.
Not Quite Snow White Written by Ashley Franklin Illustrated by Ebony Glenn	Identity Diversity Justice Action	• Students will ask and answer questions about key details in a text. • Students will acknowledge differences in the points of view of characters. • Students will describe how characters in a story respond to major events and challenges. • Students will compare and contrast the adventures and experiences of characters in stories.
Our Favorite Day of the Year Written by A. E. Ali Illustrated by Rahele Jomepour Bell	Identity Diversity	• Students will ask and answer questions about key details in a text. • Students will acknowledge differences in the points of view of characters. • Students will compare and contrast the adventures and experiences of characters in stories.
Saturday Written and illustrated by Oge Mora	Identity Diversity	• Students will ask and answer questions about key details in a text. • Students will acknowledge differences in the points of view of characters. • Compare and contrast the adventures and experiences of characters in stories.
Separate Is Never Equal Written and Illustrated by Duncan Tonatiuh	Identity Diversity Justice Action	• Students will ask and answer questions about key details in a text. • Students will acknowledge differences in the points of view of characters. • Students will describe how characters in a story respond to major events and challenges.

Book Title	Learning for Justice Standards	Literacy Standards
Sometimes People March Written and illustrated by Tessa Allen	Identity Diversity Justice Action	• Students will ask and answer questions about key details in a text. • Students will acknowledge differences in the points of view of characters. • Students will describe how characters in a story respond to major events and challenges. • Students will compare and contrast the adventures and experiences of characters in stories.
The Gift of Ramadan Written by Rabiah York Lumbard Illustrated by Laura K. Horton	Identity Diversity	• Students will ask and answer questions about key details in a text. • Students will acknowledge differences in the points of view of characters. • Students will compare and contrast the adventures and experiences of characters in stories.
The Invisible Boy Written by Trudy Ludwig Illustrated by Patrice Barton	Identity Diversity Justice Action	• Students will ask and answer questions about key details in a text. • Students will acknowledge differences in the points of view of characters. • Students will describe how characters in a story respond to major events and challenges. • Students will compare and contrast the adventures and experiences of characters in stories.
The Nian Monster Written by Andrea Wang Illustrated by Alina Chau	Identity Diversity	• Students will ask and answer questions about key details in a text. • Students will acknowledge differences in the points of view of characters. • Students will compare and contrast the adventures and experiences of characters in stories.
The Oldest Student Written by Rita Lorraine Hubbard Illustrated by Oge Mora	Identity Diversity Justice Action	• Students will ask and answer questions about key details in a text. • Students will acknowledge differences in the points of view of characters. • Students will describe how characters in a story respond to major events and challenges. • Students will compare and contrast the adventures and experiences of characters in stories.

(Continued)

(Continued)

Book Title	Learning for Justice Standards	Literacy Standards
The Remember Balloons Written by Jessie Oliveros Illustrated by Dana Wulfekotte	Identity Diversity	• Students will ask and answer questions about key details in a text. • Students will acknowledge differences in the points of view of characters. • Students will describe how characters in a story respond to major events and challenges. • Students will compare and contrast the adventures and experiences of characters in stories.
The Shadow in the Moon: A Tale of the Mid-Autumn Festival Written by Christina Matula Illustrated by Pearl Law	Identity Diversity	• Students will ask and answer questions about key details in a text. • Students will acknowledge differences in the points of view of characters. • Students will compare and contrast the adventures and experiences of characters in stories.
Tomatoes for Neela Written by Padma Lakshmi Illustrated by Juana Martinez-Neal	Identity Diversity	• Students will ask and answer questions about key details in a text. • Students will acknowledge differences in the points of view of characters.
We Are Still Here! Written by Traci Sorell Illustrated by Frane Lessac	Identity Diversity Justice Action	• Students will ask and answer questions about key details in a text. • Students will acknowledge differences in the points of view of characters. • Students will describe how characters in a story respond to major events and challenges.
We Are Water Protectors Written by Carole Lindstrom Illustrated by Michaela Goade	Identity Diversity Justice Action	• Students will ask and answer questions about key details in a text. • Students will identify words and phrases in stories or poems that suggest feelings or appeal to the senses.
We Want to Go to School! The Fight for Disability Rights By Maryann Cocca-Leffler and Janine Leffler	Identity Diversity Justice Action	• Students will ask and answer questions about key details in a text. • Students will acknowledge differences in the points of view of characters. • Students will describe how characters in a story respond to major events and challenges. • Students will compare and contrast the adventures and experiences of characters in stories.

Book Title	Learning for Justice Standards	Literacy Standards
When Aidan Became a Brother Written by Kyle Lukoff	Identity Diversity Justice Action	• Students will ask and answer questions about key details in a text. • Students will acknowledge differences in the points of view of characters. • Students will compare and contrast the adventures and experiences of characters in stories. • Students will describe how characters in a story respond to major events and challenges.
Where Are You From? Written by Yamile Saied Méndez Illustrated by Jaime Kim	Identity Diversity	• Students will ask and answer questions about key details in a text. • Students will acknowledge differences in the points of view of characters. • Students will compare and contrast the adventures and experiences of characters in stories. • Students will describe how characters in a story respond to major events and challenges.
Where Three Oceans Meet Written by Rajani LaRocca Illustrated by Archana Sreenivasan	Identity Diversity	• Students will ask and answer questions about key details in a text. • Students will acknowledge differences in the points of view of characters. • Students will compare and contrast the adventures and experiences of characters in stories.
Your Name Is a Song Written by Jamilah Thompkins-Bigelow Illustrated by Luisa Uribe	Identity Diversity Justice Action	• Students will ask and answer questions about key details in a text. • Students will acknowledge differences in the points of view of characters. • Students will describe how characters in a story respond to major events and challenges.

References

Beers, K., & Probst, E. (2017). *Disrupting thinking: Why how we read matters: Why how we read matters.* Scholastic.

Bishop, R. S. (1990). Mirrors, windows, and sliding glass doors. *Choosing and Using Books for the Classroom, 6*(3).

Chenoweth, R. (2019, September 5). Rudine Sims Bishop: "Mother" of multicultural children's literature. *Osu.Edu.* https://ehe.osu.edu/news/listing/rudine-sims-bishop-diverse-childrens-books/

Duursma, E., Augustyn, M., & Zuckerman, B. (2008). Reading aloud to children: The evidence. *Archives of Disease in Childhood, 93*(7), 554–557.

Fountas, I. C., & Pinnell, G. S. (1996). *Guided reading: Good first teaching for all children.* Heinemann.

Gold, J., & Gibson, A. (2001). *Reading aloud to build comprehension. Reading Rockets.* https://www.readingrockets.org/article/reading-aloud-build-comprehension (Originally published by Northwest Education)

Hammond, Z. L. (2015). *Culturally responsive teaching and the brain: Promoting authentic engagement and rigor among culturally and linguistically diverse students.* Corwin.

Kindle, K. J. (2009). Vocabulary development during read-alouds: Primary practices. *The Reading Teacher, 63*(3), 202–211.

Learning for Justice. (2021). *Social justice standards.* https://www.learningforjustice.org/frameworks/social-justice-standards

Neumann, S. B., Copple, C., & Bredekamp, S. (2000). *Learning to read and write: Developmentally appropriate practices for young children.* National Association for the Education of Young Children.

Newton, E., Padak, N. D., & Rasinski, T. V. (2008). *Evidence-based instruction in reading: A professional development guide to vocabulary.* Pearson Education.

Rice University. (n.d.). *Diversity defined.* https://canvas.rice.edu/courses/252/pages/diversity-defined

Index

A SAGE Publishing Company

CORWIN HAS ONE MISSION: to enhance education through intentional professional learning.

We build long-term relationships with our authors, educators, clients, and associations who partner with us to develop and continuously improve the best evidence-based practices that establish and support lifelong learning.

Because...
ALL TEACHERS ARE LEADERS

**DOMINIQUE SMITH,
DOUGLAS FISHER, NANCY FREY**

Take an active approach toward disrupting the negative effects of labels and assumptions that interfere with student learning.

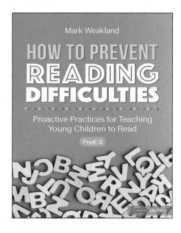

MARK WEAKLAND

Build on decades of evidence and years of experience to understand how the brain learns to read and how to apply that understanding to Tier 1 instruction.

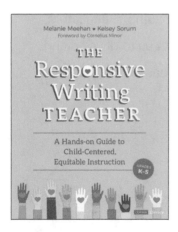

MELANIE MEEHAN, KELSEY SORUM

Learn how to adapt curriculum to meet the needs of the whole child. Each chapter offers intentional steps for responsive instruction across four domains: academic, linguistic, cultural, and social-emotional.

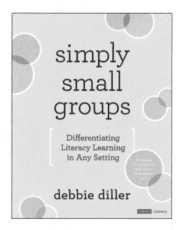

DEBBIE DILLER

Discover concrete guidance for tailoring the small-group experience to literacy instruction in order to give every reader a pathway to success.

To order your copies, visit corwin.com/literacy

At Corwin Literacy we have put together a collection of just-in-time, classroom-tested, practical resources from trusted experts that allow you to quickly find the information you need when you need it.

DOUGLAS FISHER, NANCY FREY, NICOLE LAW

Using a structured, three-pronged approach—skill, will, and thrill—students experience reading as a purposeful act with this new comprehensive model of reading instruction.

PAM KOUTRAKOS

Packed with ready-to-go lessons and tools, this user-friendly resource provides ways to weave together different aspects of literacy using one mentor text.

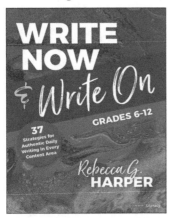

REBECCA G. HARPER

Customizable strategies turn students' informal writing into a springboard for daily writing practice in every content area—with a focus on academic vocabulary, summarizing, and using textual evidence.

MELANIE MEEHAN, CHRISTINA NOSEK, MATTHEW JOHNSON, DAVE STUART JR., MATTHEW R. KAY

This series offers actionable answers to your most pressing questions about teaching reading, writing, and ELA.

CORWIN

CLN21850